DISCOVER JOY
Studies in
Philippians

Discover Joy

Studies in Philippians

LIVING STUDIES
Tyndale House Publishers, Inc., Wheaton, Illinois

Scripture references marked TLB are taken by
permission from *The Living Bible* (© 1971, Tyndale
House Publishers, Inc., Wheaton, Illinois). Those
marked KJV are taken from the King James
Version, NASB from the *New American Standard
Bible,* NIV from the *New International Version.*

Discover Joy: Studies in Philippians was originally
published under the title: *Philippians: The
Believer's Joy in Christ.*

Second printing, December 1983

Library of Congress Catalog Card Number
82-51292
ISBN 0-8423-0606-4
Copyright © 1980 by James T. Draper, Jr.
All rights reserved
Printed in the United States of America

To Marilyn Novak
whose love for our Lord
and his Word inspires me daily,
and whose careful diligence
has prepared this and many other
manuscripts for publication

CONTENTS

1

Fellowship
of the Gospel
Philippians 1:1-5

THE BOOK OF PHILIPPIANS is a challenging treatise pointing specifically to a church that had become what every church ought to be. Much of the writing of the New Testament is written to admonish Christians to live for Christ, but in Philippians the Apostle Paul could say, "Here is an example." As we read this book and feel the heart-throb of the Apostle Paul for these Philippians Christians, we realize how far short we come of being the kind of church we ought to be.

The founding of the Philippian church is recorded in Acts 16. The Apostle Paul had come to Asia Minor by the leading of the Holy Spirit. As he walked along by the sea in Troas one night, he saw a vision of a man standing across the sea in Macedonia and saying, "Come over and help us." Perceiving that this was a message from God, "immediately we endeavored to go into Macedonia" (Acts 16:10, KJV).

They began to travel along the Egnatian Way, which ran the length of the empire, all the way to Rome. The first city they came to was Philippi, where Paul started Europe's first church. Upon arriving in a city, Paul usually went to the synagogue first. But there evidently being no synagogue in Philippi, he went down by the river, where a group of women were having a prayer meeting. He worshiped with them and shared the gospel with them. Lydia, the first convert in Europe, was very aggressive in her faith and soon led her entire household, both family and servants, to the Lord. It was a time of great rejoicing. Paul and those with him continued to share Christ in Philippi over a period of time.

One young girl, filled with demonic spirits, was a fortune-teller. After a while, she began to follow the Apostle Paul and his group around, saying, "These men are prophets of God. Listen to them. God has sent them here." Apparently the Apostle Paul did not want confirmation from such a questionable source, and didn't particularly appreciate her support. Besides that, he wanted to free her from the demons that bound her, and he did just that. This created no little stir. The owners of the girl, who had now lost their income, had Paul and Silas arrested and thrown in jail, where they were cruelly beaten and then brought before the magistrate. They were accused of upsetting the whole city and of opposing the Roman Empire. As the brave preachers began to sing and to pray in jail, a great earthquake came and set them free. The jailer, assuming the prisoners had all escaped, was about to kill himself when Paul spoke up. "We are still here. Do yourself no harm." As a result of this incident, the jailer, his family, and his servants were all converted that night.

The next day, the Apostle Paul announced that he and Silas were Roman citizens. Philippi was a colony city and thus was a miniature of the capital city. Everyone who was a Roman citizen living in Philippi had the same privileges as the citizens living in Rome. There were many privileges that went along with being a Roman citizen. He didn't have to pay taxes. He could own property. He certainly was not to be beaten and thrown in jail. So the leaders of the city set Paul and Silas free. The Apostle Paul then demanded a public apology, a public vindication, which he received but was also asked to leave as quickly as he could. So after staying a few days with Lydia and her household, Paul and Silas moved on.

The conversion of Lydia, the slave girl, and the jailer and his household—this was the beginning of the church at Philippi, a church which maintained close relationship with the Apostle Paul. Perhaps ten to twelve years elapsed between the time the church was established and the writing of this letter. Over this entire period of time, the church at Philippi had loved the apostle, had corresponded with him, had sent gifts and offerings to him, had loved him dearly. The occasion of Paul's writing this letter was to express thanks for their sending him a gift.

The apostle is writing from prison. Some think he was in prison at Caesarea Philippi, some in prison at Rome. The traditional view is that he was in Rome. At any rate we know that he was in prison and humanly speaking had every right to be in despair. A great deal of disappointment and uncertainty surrounded his life at this time. Yet the book of Philippians is a masterpiece of joy.

There are two keys to this letter. The first is the word "rejoice." "Rejoice in the Lord alway: again I say, Rejoice" (Phil. 4:4, KJV). The second idea, and the most interesting to me, is that there are about fifty references to Jesus Christ, and that makes for tremendous joy. That makes sense. If we would center our lives in Jesus Christ, we would have more joy. These are the two main themes that run through this book.

The letter opens: "Paul and Timotheus, the servants of Jesus Christ, to all the saints in Christ Jesus which are at Philippi, with the bishops and deacons: Grace be unto you, and peace, from God our Father, and from the Lord Jesus Christ. I thank my God upon every remembrance of you, always in every prayer of mine for you all making request with joy, for your fellowship in the gospel from the first day until now" (1:1-5, KJV).

THE RECIPIENTS

The recipients of this message are identified as "saints in Christ Jesus who are in Philippi, with the bishops and deacons." "Saints" is a word which literally means "holy ones," those who are holy in Jesus Christ. The Jews saw themselves as holy ones, separate ones. So, just to be sure that his readers did not take this as a purely Jewish connotation, Paul says, "saints in Christ Jesus." The source of their holiness was Christ.

The New Testament calls all believers saints. We don't like to think of ourselves as saints, but the word simply means to be separated to God, to be separated for a holy purpose. It particularly carries with it the idea of consecration, dedication. When something was sacrificed on a Jewish altar, it was set apart for the purposes of God. Once the lamb was chosen by the priest who would make the sacrifice, there would be a mark or a seal placed upon the lamb. That seal said, "You are uniquely dedicated, consecrated, separated, set apart for God's purposes." God declares that we are "sealed with that holy Spirit of promise" (Eph. 1:13, KJV). Every child of God needs to be aware of his holy and high standing before God. We are "holy ones," set apart for the purposes of God's kingdom.

Paul was writing to *all* the saints, including the bishops and deacons. "Bishops" (note the plural) is "overseers." While there was in the New Testament church a pastor who seemed to be in charge, to give guidance and direction, there was also multiple ministry at the level of the bishops and the elders.

THE REWARD

"Grace be unto you, and peace, from God our Father, and from the Lord Jesus Christ." The reward of knowing Jesus Christ is "grace" and "peace." We receive God's grace, which produces peace in our lives. The idea of peace does not mean absence of strife or perfect calm. It means perfect fulfillment, complete joy, complete realization of the intentions of God in our lives. We may be in the midst of turmoil, but God still gives us peace in our souls and hearts.

God is the only source of this peace. We say we believe this, but how many times have we thought that if we had a newer car or a different place to live, if our job payed a little bit more, we would have more peace? A man in Oklahoma told me recently, "As of right now, I have everything I thought I would ever want. I am making the salary I thought would make everything great. But I have found out that I have the same problems I had before I had the money. I am the same person." Peace comes only from walking in fellowship with God, from being in harmony with him.

". . . God our Father . . . the Lord Jesus Christ." Paul equates Christ and God. "Lord" is his name of dominance and kingship. "Jesus" is his human name, representing his ability to save men from their sins. "Christ" is his eternal name, meaning "the anointed one, the Messiah." He is the One God has sent to bring his peace into this world. This is the reward of all who are saved.

THE REMEMBRANCE

"I thank my God upon every remembrance of you" (1:3, KJV). That is an astonishing statement. Paul is saying, "I can't think of anything unpleasant about you. I can't think of one thing that I am unhappy about when I think about you. Every remembrance causes me to thank God." He couldn't say that about the church at Galatia. "O foolish Galatians, who hath bewitched you?" (Gal. 3:1, KJV). He couldn't say that of the church at Corinth. "And I, brethren, could not speak unto you as unto spiritual, but as unto carnal" (1 Cor. 3:1, KJV).

But to the church at Philippi he said, "Every memory I have of you is happy." Wouldn't it be wonderful if we so lived, loved, and served God together that as we gathered moment by moment, day by day, week by week, until Jesus comes, we would be able to say, "I thank God upon every remembrance of you." The apostle felt this way toward this church because this church had stood with him, had loved him, had provided for him, had prayed for him.

I suppose that the greatest testing the Apostle Paul had was loneliness. He was often alone, often forsaken by those around him. Yet this church had never forsaken him. When he needed encouragement, the church at Philippi had sent Epaphroditus to comfort him.

We need each other. We need the encouragement, the love, the fellowship of each other. It is a tremendous thing when we can link memory with friendship and so experience gratitude and joy. Paul loved the Philippians because of what they had shared with him.

He declares, "I thank *my* God"—not just "God," but "my God." In the moment of the most tender association with God, when God is not just a great being to worship, but is intimately involved with him, the apostle says, "I thank him for you. When he is *my* God, when he walks with me in close association, I thank him for you." We can imagine the joy that must have filled the Philippians' hearts when Paul said, "When I am closest to God, I think about you with joy."

THE REJOICING

"When I pray for you, my heart is full of joy" (1:4, TLB). After he has told them he remembers them with happiness, he says that he is continually praying for them. It would revolutionize our churches if we thus lifted each other to the throne of grace.

"For your fellowship in the gospel . . ." (1:5, KJV). They were moving in the same direction Paul was moving, they shared his dream. He wanted to spread the gospel around the world; so did they. He wanted to see that people were saved everywhere he went; so did they. If he preached, they were there to encourage him and participate in what he was doing. When money was needed, they generously and joyfully gave to provide what was needed. Whatever was important to the minister was important to the people. They moved together, they lived together, they served together. No wonder he could say, "I thank my God upon every remembrance of you." They shared his vision.

"Making request with joy, for your fellowship in the gospel." Their participation in the gospel caused him to pray happily. Sometimes we pray for people with tears. There may be a burden, a heartache, an estrangement, a breach of fellowship. With tears we pray over a wayward son or daughter, or a broken relationship. Other times we pray with trembling. But the Apostle Paul says, "Because of your commitment to God, when I pray about you I rejoice."

We can imagine the liberty that gave to him. How hard it is to pray with tears or brokenness, or trembling of soul. But because of the joy he felt, Paul could pray in freedom for them. He could call their names to God without regret and with wonderful love because of what God had done in their midst. What a wonderful time Paul had praying for a church like this.

"When I pray for you, my heart is full of joy, because of all your wonderful help in making known the Good News about Christ from the time you first heard it until now" (1:4, 5, TLB). It is not too likely that a person will be enthusiastic for God unless he starts out enthusiastically. If one starts out lukewarm, he may never heat up. Paul said, "It was exciting to see that from the first day of your conversion, you have shared this dream with me." Some start out well, but they don't finish well. "You did run well; who did hinder you?" (Gal. 5:7, KJV). The Philippian believers had great spiritual stamina. They did not slow down. He said, "You participated in the gospel on the first day and you are still doing it." It had been ten or twelve years, and they were still going strong. Today we need people with spiritual stamina, who love God and will not let up, will not slack off but move on, running well the race that is set before them.

2 The Perfecting Work of God
Philippians 1:6-8

"AND I AM SURE that God who began the good work within you will keep right on helping you grow in his grace until his task within you is finally finished on that day when Jesus Christ returns. How natural it is that I should feel as I do about you, for you have a very special place in my heart. We have shared together the blessings of God, both when I was in prison and when I was out, defending the truth and telling others about Christ. Only God knows how deep is my love and longing for you—with the tenderness of Jesus Christ" (1:6-8, TLB).

Only God knows how many times the Apostle Paul had thought about his friends in Philippi. He had gone through much loneliness, fostered and forced upon him by suffering, imprisonment, and persecution. Doubtless, many times he had brightened the dark nights with his thoughts of those Christians in Philippi. We ought to work hard at building good memories. We ought to work hard at the relationships we share and the fellowship we enjoy together. We never know when we will need to call upon our memories to bring encouragement to our hearts.

ITS CERTAINTY
"And I am sure that God who began the good work within you will keep right on helping you grow in his grace until

his task within you is finally finished on that day when Jesus Christ returns" (1:6, TLB). Here we see the certainty of the perfecting work of God. The word translated "sure" appears in numerous places in the New Testament and always means personal certainty, assurance. Paul says, "I am certain about one thing: God started a work in you and he will continue it." God will perfect that which he has begun. This is not speaking of salvation. That is certainly true, but that is not consistent to the passage. The context is: "God gave a vision to you of winning this world to Christ. You are a participant in the gospel through my ministry. I know that God is going to make sure that you complete and perfect that work."

God never starts something that he doesn't finish. God does not do anything halfway. He does not give a bird wings without giving him air to fly in. He does not give us lungs without air to breathe. There are no half measures with God. Whatever God gives, he always provides the means to use it to its fullest.

In talking to the Galatians, who were so easily led astray, Paul said, "Are ye so foolish? having begun in the Spirit, are ye made perfect by the flesh?" (Gal. 3:3, KJV). The word "begun" is the same word used here. In Galatians Paul was dealing with salvation. God began a work of grace in them through his Spirit, and the flesh cannot perfect it. We cannot be saved unless God plants his Spirit in us. There must be a divine initiative, a divine enabling in everything we would do for God.

There is no work for God that we can do in our own strength. If God is not doing his work through us, then we are not doing the work of God. We may be very religious, but the work of God is the work of *God*. It is God's work in us. How many times we have said we were going to do something but did not do it. We said we were going to be soul-winners. Why are we not doing it? It may be that we determined to do a good work for God in our own strength. Perhaps we were trying to witness for Christ out of a sense of duty or debt. Maybe we were beginning a good work in our own lives rather than asking God to give us a broken heart and a oneness with him so that he could love, serve, and minister through us.

God does not want our best. He wants his best in us. Our best is fickle. It blows hot then cold, up then down. Its only consistency is its inconsistency. But when God begins a work in us, he will keep on doing it until the day Christ Jesus returns.

The word "perform" (KJV) means "completed." Whatever work God began, he will see that it does what it is intended to do. He will perform it until the "day when Jesus Christ returns" (TLB). When we come to the place where we desperately want what God wants for our lives and do what we do because God has begun it in us, then we can be sure that God will complete that work.

ITS COMPASSION

"How natural it is that I should feel as I do about you, for you have a very special place in my heart. We have shared together the blessings of God, both when I was in prison and when I was out, defending the truth and telling others about Christ" (1:7, TLB). Nothing greater could be said of us than that we have each other in our hearts. Not in our heads, but in our hearts where we can love and care for each other, where we can praise God for each other and rejoice with each other.

Paul had them in his heart because "We have shared together the blessings of God, both when I was in prison and when I was not." At one period of early church history, one Christian visiting or sympathizing with another in jail could be thrown in jail himself. It was not always easy and was often dangerous for Christians to share in others' imprisonment and bonds. The Philippians had cared for Paul and provided for him and loved him at the risk of great danger to themselves.

He had them in his heart also because they stood with him in "defending the truth and telling others about Christ." He may have been speaking of the defense he made for the gospel before such magistrates as King Agrippa or Felix. But the idea of "defence and confirmation" (KJV) is basically that of stating a good case against an accuser. Paul is saying, "When I was accused, when my gospel was called into question, you stood by me. You spoke a good word in my defense." Today there is little of that kind of loyalty. We are quick to believe the worst about the people we respect the most.

"We have shared together the blessings of God." "Shared together" is one compound word in the Greek. The main word is *"koinonia,"* usually translated "fellowship." It means to "become involved with, to be in compliance with, to share whatever comes upon another." The combination of the two words together makes a strong word of union for a common purpose, a word of love and compassion for a common goal. It refers to pushing aside personal prejudices and whatever else might divide and separate. It means being involved together for the gospel.

"The blessings of God" refers both to imprisonment and to preaching the gospel. He is saying, "When I was in prison, God gave me great blessings and you shared in it. You were part of the grace of God upon me when I was in prison. When I was defending the gospel, God gave grace for that and you were partakers in that. Whatever the pressure, whatever the point of need, God brought blessing, and you were part of it. God used you to be a part of the blessings which he gave to me in my imprisonment and in my preaching." Wouldn't it be wonderful if we could look at each other and know that every time there was a need pressing in on our hearts, other Christians were sharing in God's grace for us at that hour.

ITS COMPULSION

"Only God knows how deep is my love and longing for you—with the tenderness of Jesus Christ" (1:8, TLB). The King James Version says, "I long after you all in the bowels of Jesus Christ." The Greek word translated "bowels" means "the seat of tenderness, the seat of emotion." It had nothing to do with anatomy. It speaks of genuine love and deep compassion. Today we might say, "I long for you all with the heart of Jesus Christ." In verse 7 Paul said, "I have you in my heart." In verse 8 he said, "I long for you with Christ's heart." What he is saying is, "I have you in my heart, and Christ has you in his heart." Paul felt compelled to love the Philippians as Jesus loved them.

"The tenderness of Jesus Christ" is a metaphor in the original language which speaks of perfect union. The love of Jesus Christ was put inside Paul like a hand in a glove, so that when that hand reached out to them it was not the Apostle Paul reaching, but Jesus. When he loved them, Jesus was loving them through him. When he wrote to them, they heard his message not as a word from Paul, but a word from Jesus through Paul.

By saying "God is my record," the Apostle Paul was saying he was deadly serious about this. He was letting them know that what he was about to say was very important. God witnessed to his "love and longing" for them. "Longing" speaks of homesickness. He wanted them to know how much he missed and loved them. One reason the early church grew so rapidly and turned the world upside down was because of the loyalty of Christians to each other and to their Lord. If we had that kind of loyalty, we couldn't build buildings large enough to hold the people that would want to be a part of our fellowship. The truth is, we are largely strangers one to another. We resist attempts to get closer to each other. We don't want to love, perhaps for fear of being rejected or torn apart.

What Paul and the Philippians shared was something that distance couldn't destroy. Whether they were together or apart, there was a deep compulsion to encourage and lift each other up, and God honored that spirit in a tremendous way.

A Life
That Excels
Philippians 1:9-11

"MY PRAYER FOR YOU is that you will overflow more and more with love for others, and at the same time keep on growing in spiritual knowledge and insight, for I want you always to see clearly the difference between right and wrong, and to be inwardly clean, no one being able to criticize you from now until our Lord returns. May you always be doing those good, kind things which show that you are a child of God, for this will bring much praise and glory to the Lord" (1:9-11, TLB).

Paul doesn't pray that the Philippians will love each other or that they will love him. They already do that. Rather, he prays that their love may be channeled in the right direction, that it may be kept from selfish and impure motives.

THE DEPTH

"My prayer for you is that you will overflow more and more with love for others." Nothing would satisfy the Apostle Paul short of full Christian maturity. "I do not want your love to be shallow or incomplete. I want your love to abound more and more, to move on toward perfection and maturity. I want it to be a love that deepens and deepens until it is grounded totally on the love of Jesus Christ."

It is right for us to pray that our love for each other will deepen and mature. We should pray that we learn to love each other in the very spirit and love of Christ.

THE DISCERNMENT

"At the same time keep on growing in spiritual knowledge and insight, for I want you always to see clearly the difference between right and wrong." The word "knowledge" is an interesting compound word. The Greek word for "knowledge" was *gnosis*, which simply means knowledge, fact, or information. One could have a false *gnosis*, a false knowledge. But Paul puts a little preposition on the word, making it *epignosis*, "full knowledge." It describes an individual who gathers all the facts and looks them all over carefully. He has full, complete knowledge.

Paul prays that the Philippians' love will abound more and more until they have a full knowledge, a full understanding. He ties this to "insight" or "judgment" (KJV). This involves making decisions, judging the value of something.

We all face choices and render judgments. We all have to make decisions. The wise person understands that his ultimate choice is not between good and evil, but between the good and the best. This takes discernment. How can we keep from wasting our time with good significant things that are not crucial or vital? How do we stop being a slave to the "urgent" and dwell upon the important?

"I want you always to see clearly the difference between right and wrong." This is putting into practice the knowledge and discernment already mentioned. If we have this perfect knowledge and this keen discernment, we will put it into action. Christian principle is not only something to know, but to do. Christianity is not a way of assimilating facts. Christianity is a way of living, of facing life and the opportunities that are before us. It is not only a way of doing religious things, but also a way of relating to our families, working during the week, going to school. It is a way of life!

"See clearly" means "to confirm, to test and make sure" that something is true. A literal translation of that would be, "approve the things that differ." Paul again underscores the fine line between the good and the best. This is a challenge to live a life that excels. We are to rise above the average, to reach above mediocrity, and strive for that which is excellent. "They that wait upon the Lord . . . shall mount up with wings as eagles" (Isa. 40:31, KJV). The eagle climbs to the heights. He soars upon the wings of the heavens. His home is in the pure, clean atmosphere of the heavens of this earth. When you wait on God and walk in his power, you enjoy a life that rises above the ordinary, a life that touches eternity.

THE DEMONSTRATION
"I want you . . . to be inwardly clean" (1:10, TLB). The origin of the word translated "inwardly clean" ("sincere," KJV) is difficult to find, but without any question it speaks of purity, a transparency of life in our relationship with God, right relationship with God. Our lives must be open to God's Holy Spirit. He will, thus, at our invitation bring cleansing and forgiveness so we can walk in purity and sincerity of life.

Then Paul says, "no one being able to criticize you." The King James Version translates this "without offence." The idea is that of not being offensive to others. Our relationship to God is vertical, our relationship to man horizontal. Both are depicted by the cross on which Jesus died.

The cross brings man together with man and man together with God. Paul is saying that if we have a problem with a Christian brother, we are out of fellowship with God.

Here was a church where the love of God was loving through them to each other. They had such deep love that they were caring for each other, lifting each other up, hurting with each other, laughing and crying with each other, praising each other, rejoicing together. What a holy hilarity there was in the fellowship of that church. This was to continue "until our Lord returns."

"May you always be doing those good, kind things which show that you are a child of God" (1:11, TLB). This is a perfect passive participle. In English, tense means time. In the Greek, tense means condition. It speaks of a *kind* of action, not a time of action. The perfect tense in the Greek doesn't simply mean something that is in the past, but a past action that still stands as having been done now. If we have this kind of relationship with God, we will "always be doing those good, kind things that show we are children of God." When we walk in fellowship with God, we have already been filled with the "good, kind things" that right relationships with God produce. The fruit tree doesn't make the fruit grow, it simply lets the fruit grow. It requires no effort at all on the part of the tree. By its life, it produces fruit. In the same way, when we choose that which is excellent and live a life for Christ that rises above the average, we will bear "the fruits of righteousness" (KJV) in our lives.

This kind of living comes "through Jesus Christ" (NASB). We can only live that kind of life through Christ. We try our best to be good Christians, but our best is not enough. We are going to always lie, cheat, have evil thoughts. Our best is filthy rags. God wants *his* best in us, his righteousness produced through us. "Let this mind be in you, which was also in Christ Jesus" (2:5, KJV). Paul didn't say, "Think like Jesus." He said, "Let Jesus think through you." Christianity isn't just dwelling on biblical principles and truths and indoctrinating ourselves to react like Christians. Christianity is a planting of the seed of the gospel in our hearts and allowing God to live his life through us. This comes only through Jesus Christ.

Notice that phrase, "unto the glory and praise of God" (1:11, KJV). God's working through us always brings honor to him. One of the great tragedies in this century is that we give so much honor, so much credit, so much praise to each other, rather than to God. "To God be the glory, great things *he* hath done."

4

An Unexpected Result
Philippians 1:12-14

"AND I WANT YOU to know this, dear brothers: Everything that has happened to me here has been a great boost in getting out the Good News concerning Christ. For everyone around here, including all the soldiers over at the barracks, knows that I am in chains simply because I am a Christian. And because of my imprisonment many of the Christians here seem to have lost their fear of chains! Somehow my patience has encouraged them and they have become more and more bold in telling others about Christ" (1:12-14, TLB).

Since Paul was in prison, the Philippians were concerned about him. We can be sure they were praying and trusting God to provide for him. But since he was in jail, they probably assumed things were not going too well. In this passage of Scripture we see an unusual result of Paul's imprisonment. Instead of his imprisonment stopping the gospel, it had done just the opposite. Instead of closing doors, it had opened doors, so much so that he could write, "Everyone around here...knows that I am in chains simply because I am a Christian." And, "All the saints salute you, chiefly they that are of Caesar's household" (4:22, KJV). The gospel had penetrated into the very depths of the imperial city.

It is not faith's task to explain things, but to overcome them. It is not faith's responsibility to give us logical explanations for all the difficulties that we encounter, but to give us the wisdom from God to use whatever difficulty there may be to shape our lives. Indeed, the greatest witness of faith, even in our day, is the witness of old age and adversity. The Apostle Paul is coming to the end of his life and is imprisoned for his faith. Yet he is still looking forward. Great is the faith of those who are advanced in years, who have passed through the wars of life, who have walked through difficulties and circumstances that could overwhelm them. Though they may face death, as the Apostle Paul did when he wrote this, yet their faith looks beyond! That is the design of the gospel—to produce a faith that ever stretches forth, that reaches beyond the circumstances.

The phrase "dear brothers" identified the Philippians as co-workers with Paul. They were on the same team, working toward the same goal. They were brothers in Christ.

THE CIRCUMSTANCES

"Everything that has happened to me here has been a great boost in getting out the Good News concerning Christ." Or as the King James Version says, "The things which happened unto me have fallen out rather for the furtherance of the gospel." How could a man who was in prison, closely guarded all the time, say his circumstances produced progress for the gospel? "For the hope of Israel I am bound with this chain" (Acts 28:20). "I am an ambassador in bonds" (Eph. 6:20). The Greek word for "chain" described the short chain that a Roman soldier would use to keep a prisoner close to him. If we study the word the Apostle Paul used in Philippians and Ephesians, we discover some specifics of his imprisonment.

In Acts 28:16 we discover that when Paul came to Rome,

he was allowed to rent himself quarters in which to live. He stayed in a place that he paid for himself with his guard. Evidently when he came to Rome, he was handed over to the captain of the praetorian guard, and was then chained to a soldier. He provided his own lodging, but he also had a soldier chained to him by a short chain fastening his wrist to the soldier's wrist.

Can we imagine being chained twenty-four hours a day to a soldier? They changed guards several times each day, so we can see how it would be very easy for all of the guards in a particular brigade to know what was happening to the Apostle Paul. And as he witnessed to those about him, the guards would hear it all too.

Some might view this as discouraging and restrictive. He was never by himself, never free to do anything without a guard being there. Yet Paul said that his circumstances had turned out to be a "great boost" (1:12, TLB) to his ministry.

The word translated "great boost" (King James Version, "furtherance") was used to describe the progress of an army. It referred to clearing out the undergrowth, to chopping down trees and removing barriers in the way of the army. Many times when an army marched through a country, they would come to vast wildernesses and would be hampered by thick underbrush. An advance guard would be sent out to cut away the underbrush and the trees that were in the way, so that the army could march by unhindered. Rather than hindering the gospel, Paul's imprisonment had done just the opposite. He was saying, "Rather than stopping the gospel, my imprisonment has actually been for the good of the gospel. The gospel has made more progress with me in jail than it would have any other way."

God is master of circumstances. Whatever our situation, however dark it may appear, however bleak it may seem to us, God is still able to use it to bring great progress to the message of his gospel.

"All things work together for good to them that love God, to them who are the called according to his purpose" (Rom. 8:28, KJV). Whatever the circumstances, God is in control. Whether it be a physical handicap or weakness, a material discouragement or disappointment, or a social or interpersonal difficulty, he is able to bless. We are talking about a faith that brings victory over circumstances. When our present experience is discouraging and depressing, God can turn it around to the advantage of the cause of the gospel. Our trouble is that we are more concerned for our own personal comfort and success than we are for the preaching of the gospel of Christ. Our circumstances discourage us because we expect to see them as the criteria of our success. But Paul is saying to the church at Philippi, "Imprisonment is not what I planned or expected, but my circumstances have brought greater progress for the gospel."

All of us have circumstances we would like to change. But if we would view all of life as being within the care and the providential hand of God, we would know that whatever God allows to happen to us can be made to produce an advance for the gospel of Jesus Christ. Our part is to stand faithful in the midst of those circumstances.

THE CIRCULATION

"Everyone around here... knows that I am in chains simply because I am a Christian" (1:13, TLB). Paul was in prison because of his commitment to Jesus Christ. We do well if all our difficulties and bonds come to us as a result of our stand for Christ. "Praise the Lord if you are punished for doing right! Of course, you get no credit for being patient if you are beaten for doing wrong; but if you do right and suffer for it, and are patient beneath the blows, God is well pleased" (1 Pet. 2:19, 20). Anyone can suffer for doing wrong. If we suffer, we should suffer because Christ is our Lord and we share in the hostility shown to him. Being in prison because of Jesus is better than being pastor of any church anywhere if that is what God has called us to do.

Paul was in jail on a "bum rap." He didn't do what he was accused of doing. Some think he appealed to Caesar to get away from the prejudice and politics of Palestine. The real reason was that he believed God wanted him in Rome. A divine mandate drove him to appeal to Caesar and thus get free passage to Rome.

News circulated around Rome that here was a man who was completely consumed with the message of Jesus Christ, a missionary with a new zeal and a new message, a man who was in prison for Christ. That was the news that was circulating—not a hard luck story, but his suffering for Christ.

Even "the soldiers over at the barracks" (1:13, TLB) knew. The King James says, "in all the palace." The word is literally "praetorian" and could refer to a place or to a body of people. As to a place, the word first meant the headquarters of the general of the army. It could be a tent in the field, but wherever his headquarters were located that was the praetorian. Later it came to mean the residence of the ruler; i.e., the palace. Later still, it occasionally referred to the residence or the dwelling place of a very important person, a wealthy person. It could have been any one of the three connotations.

Here the word referred to a group of people. The praetorian guard was a very elite group of about 10,000 hand-picked soldiers. Originally they served for twelve years, but later it was stretched to sixteen years. They were the personal bodyguards of the emperor and enforced what he said.

It was to this group that the Apostle Paul was turned over when he came to Rome. The Apostle Paul was chained twenty-four hours a day to a soldier of one of the most significant groups in Roman society. For eight hours, this soldier had to listen to Paul dictate letters to churches and talk with visitors about the truth of the gospel. Some of these guards accepted Christ. After eight hours of listening to a man like Paul pray and preach and witness, the guard would unchain himself and another one would take his place. This went on for two years. We can imagine how many soldiers heard the gospel in the space of two years! The ones that weren't actually chained to Paul doubtless heard about it from others.

Paul would never have chosen these circumstances, for in his heart was a dream to go on to Spain and other areas of the world to preach the gospel. But the Holy Spirit, working among the circumstances of the apostle's imprisonment, caused the faith of the Apostle Paul to be circulated throughout the entire city of Rome. What a tremendous witness for Christ!

THE COURAGE

"And because of my imprisonment many of the Christians here seem to have lost their fear of chains! Somehow my patience has encouraged them and they have become more and more bold in telling others about Christ" (1:14, TLB).

Many Christians in Rome were discouraged because of Paul's imprisonment. They were very hesitant to share Christ, realizing the risk they faced. But when they saw what God did through the circumstances, many of these

Christians were infused with a new courage. If God could use Paul in jail, then he could use them too, whether in prison or out.

Courage spreads like wildfire. The Apostle Paul, who could easily have given up hope, continued to witness and preach even though he was chained to the soldiers who guarded him. And his courage inspired new courage in the hearts of the Christians in Rome. As we stand tall for Christ, with God's Word in our heart and upon our lips, we will encourage others to do the same.

What we do affects others. What we do is important to those who observe it. We desperately need the encouragement we can get from each other. That is why we need the church. If we stayed home and just read our Bibles, we would soon get so discouraged we wouldn't know what to do. We need each other.

"What a wonderful God we have—he is the Father of our Lord Jesus Christ, the source of every mercy, and the one who so wonderfully comforts and strengthens us in our hardships and trials. And why does he do this? So that when others are troubled, needing our sympathy and encouragement, we can pass on to them this same help and comfort God has given us. You can be sure that the more we undergo sufferings for Christ, the more he will shower us with his comfort and encouragement. We are in deep trouble for bringing you God's comfort and salvation. But in our trouble God had comforted us—and this, too, to help you: to show you from our personal experience how God will tenderly comfort you when you undergo these same sufferings. He will give you the strength to endure" (2 Cor. 1:3-7, TLB).

Everything God gives us, he gives us to give to others. He doesn't give us anything to keep. If we don't share the comfort God gives to us, we will soon lose that comfort. If we don't share the victory that God has placed in our lives, we will soon lose that victory. God wants us to share.

If we stand together, lifting each other up and sharing in the strength of God's presence in our lives, we will with a new courage move out into this world to present the gospel of Jesus Christ with power.

Preaching Christ
Philippians 1:15-18

5

"SOME, OF COURSE, are preaching the Good News because they are jealous of the way God has used me. They want reputations as fearless preachers! But others have purer motives, preaching because they love me, for they know that the Lord has brought me here to use me to defend the Truth. And some preach to make me jealous, thinking that their success will add to my sorrows here in jail! But whatever their motive for doing it, the fact remains that the Good News about Christ is being preached and I am glad" (1:15-18, TLB).

Some in Rome who were preaching with the wrong motives preached Christ to promote themselves and cause discomfort for the great apostle. Today we enjoy evaluating why people do what they do. This passage has a great deal to say to us about that.

CONTENTION

Some were preaching out of envy and strife. They carried an attitude of jealousy and divisiveness, rivalry and turmoil. They were not trying to advance the gospel, but themselves. They were selfish men, preaching out of schism and division. They wanted to divide the fellowship, thus destroying the harmony of the church. We would think that this kind of contention would certainly provoke the censure of the apostle. Surely everyone ought to preach for the right motives and with the right attitudes.

"Jealous of . . . me" was one word in the Greek and originally meant "to work for hire." It came to have a political meaning to it, referring to someone who would canvass to further his own cause, one who worked totally for selfish motives. They were not working for the kingdom, not for the brethren, but for themselves.

Paul goes on to say that their motives were not only selfish, but impure and filled with hostility and contentiousness. They wanted to "add to my sorrows here in jail" (1:17, TLB). "Sorrows" was a word which could be applied in certain instances to an irritation caused by the rubbing of an object. Some scholars think he was referring to his chains becoming an increasing irritation to him. But it is more likely that they assumed that their preaching would pull followers away from the Apostle Paul and thus isolate him from other believers. They would persuade the believers to stop supporting and loving him. So they thought that the better they did in preaching the gospel, the more it would hurt him. It is difficult to imagine a worse reason to preach the gospel.

Even today many seem to preach out of divisiveness and contention. We all have a touch of it in our lives. We are generally more excited when someone is saved in *our* fellowship than when they are saved somewhere else. Like it or not, we have fostered a spirit of competitiveness with other churches, as though we were the ones who had the corner on the truth and they are somewhat less equipped than we. We are not as excited about reaching the world as we are about doing better than someone else. That is one reason why the church today is creeping and crawling instead of marching victoriously.

COMPASSION

Notice now the compassion in Paul's spirit as he points out that not everyone was preaching with the wrong motives. Some were preaching out of goodwill, with his best interests at heart. They wanted to encourage him, help him, lift him up. They loved Paul and the gospel. They were all lifting up the same Lord; so there was a spirit of love that bound their hearts.

Certainly that should be the purpose for preaching the gospel—love, compassion, concern.

COMMUNICATION

There were two factions in Rome. One faction condemned and criticized Paul. They did everything they could to outdo him. They wanted to make his bonds more miserable. They wanted to put him down and pull away those who were loyal to him. Others supported him. They loved him and believed in what he had done. They were excited about the testimony that spread all over Rome because of his wonderful witness for Christ in chains. We have these same two factions in every church and community today.

The beginning of verse 18—"But whatever their motive . . ."—is saying in effect, "What difference does it make?" We didn't expect that. Surely he meant to say, "Shame on the bad guys. Those people with bad attitudes had better get their hearts right." Remember, Paul is not talking about false doctrine, but about people who preach the truth in the wrong way. And Paul is saying, "Why worry about his motive? As long as he proclaims the gospel of Christ, what difference does his attitude make?"

"The fact remains that the Good News about Christ is being preached and I am glad" (1:18, TLB). The communication of the gospel was the most important thing to the Apostle Paul.

"They know that the Lord has brought me here to use me to defend the Truth" (1:16, TLB). Paul is saying, "God didn't call me to defend myself. He called me to defend the gospel." Sometimes we spend so much time trying to justify ourselves and our own integrity that we have little time left over to proclaim the gospel.

Paul rated the gospel above personalities. One of the problems the church at Corinth had was that they had a party spirit. Some claimed allegiance to Apollos, some to Paul, some to Peter, some only to Christ. Paul wrote the Corinthians specifically to pull the factions together. They made too much of individual personalities. Christ was the key. All else is superfluous. He is the One who gives meaning and purpose to the body.

Here Paul is saying the same thing. He saw the defense of the gospel as above petty quarrels, above personality differences.

The Apostle Paul did indeed defend the gospel. We learn from Acts 28:16-30 that Judaizers and others came and questioned him about Jesus, debating theological truth. He indeed did defend, and, as he defended, he proclaimed the gospel. To Paul, the important thing was to communicate the gospel of Jesus Christ.

We have all had bouts with ruffled feelings, with bitterness and resentment. We have all felt sorry for ourselves and have been upset because we were slighted. But was it because of our desire to proclaim the gospel or because of our desire to vindicate ourselves?

Paul did not rejoice in others' wrong motives, or in their hostility and divisiveness. He could not praise God for their jealousy and strife. But he was glad that the gospel was being proclaimed, that the message of Christ was being preached. He was not seeking satisfaction by vindicating himself of all the rumors that were spread. His joy came in the communication of the gospel. He did not delight in being esteemed more highly than others, but in the fact that the gospel was being spread. That was how much he loved Jesus Christ and his gospel.

The Apostle Paul felt that proclaiming the gospel of Christ is the most important single achievement of the Christian community. As much as we want harmony, the most important thing is the preaching of the gospel. That was the source of the apostle's joy and fulfillment in his life.

He had a burning zeal for Jesus Christ and for the gospel. May God produce in our hearts such a burden that we will not find our joy in anything less than the presentation of the message of the Good News of Jesus Christ.

6

The
Essence
of Life
Philippians 1:19-21

"I AM GOING to keep on being glad, for I know that as you pray for me, and as the Holy Spirit helps me, this is all going to turn out for my good. For I live in eager expectation and hope that I will never do anything that will cause me to be ashamed of myself but that I will always be ready to speak out boldly for Christ while I am going through all these trials here, just as I have in the past; and that I will always be an honor to Christ, whether I live or whether I must die. For to me, living means opportunities for Christ, and dying—well, that's better yet!" (1:19-21, TLB).

THE FOUNDATION OF THIS LIFE

"I am going to keep on being glad, for I know that as you pray for me, and as the Holy Spirit helps me, this is all going to turn out for my good" (1:19, TLB).

The Greek word translated "good" means "salvation." It was the word used to speak of salvation in its simplest form—i.e., forgiveness of sins, eternal life in Jesus Christ. It can also refer to the expression of that salvation, its day-by-day application. Paul is saying that there may be those who would destroy our peace and our happiness, but they cannot—Jesus Christ is still in control. Deliverance and salvation will result from all that we are facing.

We can face life with the assurance that nothing that happens to us surprises God. Nothing comes our way that God cannot take care of. God will grant grace and strength for every need. God never asks us to board a sinking ship. God never leads us down a dead-end street. God always brings life and deliverance. If the Apostle Paul could say this while he was in prison, knowing that his days on earth were numbered, certainly we can claim it for our lives.

How is this life sustained? Paul says in verse 19 that it will occur as the Philippians pray for him and as the Holy Spirit helps him. These two elements are absolutely essential to every Christian's life.

The Apostle Paul never got too big to ask people to pray for him. He constantly reminded them that he needed their prayers. You see, the Christian life is a life that we enter into together. We desperately need each other, and none of us can stand alone. It is critical that we pray for each other—in stress, under pressure, in the midst of joy. The greatest joy and delight we have is to pray one for another.

The Apostle Paul was their leader, the one who introduced them to Christ, the one God used to establish that church. Yet he said, "I need your prayers." Everyone needs prayer, but perhaps especially ministers, because they face unbelievable responsibilities and pressure. Ministers deal with those who are dead in trespasses and sin. They handle matters of eternal life. Who of us is capable of such a challenge? Who can stand in the gap between God and man? If ever a person needed to be lifted up in prayer, it is the one who is assigned to be a minister of the gospel.

The main object of Satan's assault in the church is the pastor. If Satan can destroy the work of the ministry, he can spread his poison. Christian leaders desperately need the intercession that we can give. They need the strength that our prayers will provide. We must pray for those God has given to lead us, and we must pray for each other.

Then Paul declares that he will be delivered through the Holy Spirit. Unless God's Holy Spirit does something in our lives, we will not be faithful to what God has called us to do. The task that has been assigned to each of us cannot be achieved in human energy or human strength. If we can explain everything we do in terms of our own ingenuity and effort, we have miserably failed. We desperately need the power of the Holy Spirit in what we do.

The only time I ever get really discouraged in the church is when everything is predictable, when I know exactly what is going to happen. It is a travesty upon worship when that is true because God wants to move in fresh and unexpected ways in our lives. He wants to move in ways that we could not possibly anticipate until they happen. If we are going to maintain the freshness of our faith, to continue in the life that God has called us to live, it will be through the power of the Spirit of Jesus Christ operating in and through us. We must lay our lives open before him and claim his provision and presence in our lives.

THE ANTICIPATION OF THAT LIFE

"For I live in eager expectation and hope that I will never do anything that will cause me to be ashamed of myself but that I will always be ready to speak out boldly for Christ while I am going through all these trials here, just as I have in the past; and that I will always be an honor to Christ, whether I live or whether I must die" (1:20, TLB). This verse is speaking about public witness. The word "boldly" refers to boldness in speech. Paul is saying, "I don't want to ever be afraid to stand up for Jesus, because I know Christ will be exalted by my boldness in speaking the truth."

"Eager expectation" is a compound of three words in the original language. It means "to look away from what may be right at hand and totally concentrate on another object," or literally "from," "ahead," "to look." This is the first time in the New Testament that it appears. The Apostle Paul was the only person to use it. He may have coined the phrase.

Paul focused his attention on one particular object. His expectation, his great desire was that he would not be embarrassed by cowardice. He would stand for Jesus Christ. He would speak his name and minister publicly and boldly before others.

If every Christian fellowship was filled with people who lived for one thing, who were not ashamed to mention the name of Jesus and to be identified with Christ, who boldly stood up and witnessed for his glory, we would revolutionize this world in less time than it takes us to discuss it.

How does one exalt Jesus? The best illustration I know is that of the telescope. The telescope doesn't add anything to what is already there. It puts no new object in the sky. All it does is make it easier for us to see what is there. We don't add anything to Jesus. There is no quality in our life that will enhance the character of Jesus Christ. Our lives are to be like a telescope, something through which people can view Christ more clearly. Jesus said concerning himself, "Anyone who has seen me has seen the Father" (John 14:9). He was saying that when we see him, we are looking into the face of God. And when people see us, they should see something of Jesus Christ.

We are to live so completely devoted to the purposes of Jesus Christ, boldly standing for him, so that when people look at us, they can look through us to Jesus Christ. That is how we are to live. Our purpose is simply to exalt Jesus.

Paul says, "I look away from that which I have had my attention on and concentrate instead on never being silent in my stand for God, trusting him to give me boldness always to speak so that whether I live or die, I honor him." Life or death is not the issue. Death is just a valley through which we walk into eternity. If we were concerned that by living and by dying we exalt Jesus Christ, we would find every experience of life and death meaningful.

THE CONSUMMATION OF THIS LIFE

"For me to live is Christ, and to die is gain" (1:21, KJV). When we are working, it is for Jesus. When we are eating, it is for Jesus. When we are relaxing, it is for Jesus. When we are worshiping, it is for Jesus. When we are being kind and considerate to someone else, it is for Jesus. When we are being a friend or a comforter, it is for Jesus. Whatever we are doing, all living is through and for Jesus Christ. The Apostle Paul was a person of a single purpose, a purpose which brought unity to his life. There was only one goal for his life: to honor Christ. He had learned that Christ puts meaning into every area of life. Everything in life is made sweeter because of him. Our family is more precious if we love them in Jesus. Our work is more fulfilling if we work in Jesus. Everything we do is better if Jesus Christ is the center of our lives.

Paul is not saying that to die is better than to live. Rather, the meaning is that when we live for Christ, dying is simply a continuation and in fact a completion of the life we are living. Living for Christ, not death, is magnified here. Death is simply an extension of that experience. We walk through the valley of the shadow of death into the sunlight of eternity in a fulfilling relationship with our Savior.

To live is Christ. He is our one purpose in life. When we can look at our husbands or wives with the one aim of living for Christ, it will make a difference in our love for them. When we can look at our children or our brothers or sisters knowing that to live is Christ, it will make a difference how we relate to them. When we can look at our parents knowing that Christ is all, then it will make a difference in our lives. The same is true of our vocation, our church, our friends. When we can look at every experience and relationship of life with Christ at the center, it eliminates every possibility of despair or discouragement.

We are not ready to die until we begin to live for Christ. When we view life as a glorious opportunity to walk with Christ and view all our relationships and responsibilities as being in his presence, then we will be that telescope through which people can see the Father.

7 Confidence
in Two Worlds
Philippians 1:22-26

"BUT IF LIVING will give me more opportunities to win people to Christ, then I really don't know which is better, to live or die! Sometimes I want to live and at other times I don't, for I long to go and be with Christ. How much happier for *me* than being here! But the fact is that I can be of more help to *you* by staying! Yes, I am still needed down here and so I feel certain I will be staying on earth a little longer, to help you grow and become happy in your faith; my staying will make you glad and give you reason to glorify Christ Jesus for keeping me safe, when I return to visit you again" (1:22-26, TLB).

Paul speaks in these verses about having confidence both to live and to die. In effect, he says, "I have a civil war within me. Sometimes I want to die and sometimes I want to live." The Greek text indicates that he is absolutely rigid between two objects. He can't go right, he can't go left—he can only go straight ahead. He is really saying, "I don't have to choose whether to live or to die—I cannot move one way or the other. I can only move forward. God is the one who has to choose life or death for me."

FRUITFUL LABOR
"But the fact is that I can be of more help to *you* by staying! Yes, I am still needed down here and so I feel certain I will

be staying on earth a little longer, to help you grow and become happy in your faith" (1:24, 25, TLB). The apostle's remaining would produce fruit in them.

A barren Christian is a contradiction. God wants us to be fruitful. Jesus said, "Yes, I am the Vine; you are the branches. Whoever lives in me and I in him shall produce a large crop of fruit. For apart from me you can't do a thing. . . . You didn't choose me! I chose you! I appointed you to go and produce lovely fruit always" (John 15:5, 16, TLB). Most verses in the New Testament pointing to the sovereignty of God in choosing men reveal that he chose us to bear fruit. He predestined us to good works. That is the kind of life a Christian is to live. That is God's purpose for us.

This statement is not the cry of a man who is afraid to die and thus chooses to live. Nor is it the cry of a man who is afraid to live, so he chooses to die. It is a man who is walking with God by faith. He is not afraid of life or death, but is confident because he is walking and living in Christ. Living for Christ means serving Christ, laboring in the Lord's vineyard, bearing fruit. Christian service is fruitful labor.

FIERCE PRESSURE

"Sometimes I want to live and at other times I don't, for I long to go and be with Christ. How much happier for *me* than being here! But the fact is that I can be of more help to *you* by staying!" (1:23, 24, TLB). It is not up to Paul whether he lives or dies. It is God's power to give life and it is God's power to take life. We have absolutely no control over when we will die. Walking in God, living in him, we only move ahead under his grace and direction.

Here is the pressure: He says he has "a desire to depart" (1:23, KJV). "Depart" was a word used to describe untying the line to a tent so the tent could be taken down. In 2 Cor. 5:1 Paul says, "If our earthy house of this tabernacle [tent] were dissolved, we have a building of God, an house not made with hands, eternal in the heavens" (KJV). It is as though the Apostle Paul is saying here, "My desire is to fold this old tent and move on to my permanent mansion." He is not looking forward to death, but to what lies beyond death. He is anticipating that which God has reserved for him after death.

He says, "I long to go and be with Christ" (1:23, TLB). We don't fully understand what it means to be with Christ. Certainly it includes perfect fellowship with him, participating in his glory. Surely it means that we will be like him, perfect in all which he has sought to achieve in us. When we depart this life, we are with the Lord, and that is "far better." Every day that we live, every day that we lie down at the end of the day, we are one day closer to being with Christ.

"But...I can be of more help to *you* by staying" (1:24, TLB). He says that he was more needed here. These new Christians needed his encouragement, his ministry, his love. He loved them so much that being of service to them meant just as much to him as the desire of his heart to be with Christ.

That is something to be loved like that. We can understand something of the feeling that must have welled up in the hearts of these Christians in Philippi when they heard their beloved leader say to them, "I desire to fold my tent and move into my permanent home with God, but because I love you it is better for me to stay here."

FINAL CONFIDENCE
"Yes, I am still needed down here and so I feel certain I will be staying on earth a little longer, to help you grow and

become happy in your faith; my staying will make you glad and give you reason to glorify Christ Jesus for keeping me safe, when I return to visit you again" (1:25, 26, TLB).

Notice he says, "I feel certain...." That is confidence. The great apostle was caught between the desire of his soul to be with the Lord and his knowing he was needed to serve the Philippians. But he had this confidence that God had told him what was in the days ahead—God told him he would remain with them. The two words "abide" and "continue" (1:25, KJV) cannot be fully translated into the English language. It is a play on words. *Menien* means "to remain with," and so it is translated "I know I shall remain." *Paramenien* is translated "continue," *para* meaning "by" or "alongside." He would not only remain with them, but would be "alongside" them, to help them and encourage them. Paul was saying, "I know that I shall be here, but more than that, I will help you. I know that I will be able to assist you, stand by your side, help you in your progress and maturity, enhance your worship."

Paul had just said, "For me to live is Christ." Now he is saying, "For me to live is you." How do we reconcile that? Anyone can say, "For me to live in Christ." But if we really mean it, we will serve those whom God has given to us. We don't love Christ if we don't love those God has committed to us. Loving Jesus expresses itself in concrete evidence as we touch the lives of other people.

The confidence that the Apostle Paul expresses here is that God is going to allow him to stay on in order to be a minister to a particular people and to help them in their faith. For whom are we living? Ourselves? Our own families and friends? One thing is sure. If we are often irritated and upset, we are living for ourselves. Who is walking with God today because of us? Whose life is more like Jesus' because of us? To whom is heaven more real today because of us? If we can't answer those questions in concrete terms, then we are playing games with God.

What Paul does for the Philippians will bring honor to Jesus (1:26). We ought to pray that whatever God allows us to do will bring someone closer to God and bring honor to Jesus Christ. What do people think about when they see us coming? Do they honor Jesus and rejoice in him?

Worthy of
the Gospel
Philippians 1:27-30

8

"BUT WHATEVER HAPPENS to me, remember always to live as Christians should, so that, whether I ever see you again or not, I will keep on hearing good reports that you are standing side by side with one strong purpose—to tell the Good News fearlessly, no matter what your enemies may do. They will see this as a sign of their downfall, but for you it will be a clear sign from God that he is with you, and that he has given you eternal life with him. For to you has been given the privilege not only of trusting him but also of suffering for him. We are in this fight together. You have seen me suffer for him in the past; and I am still in the midst of a great and terrible struggle now, as you know so well" (1:27-30, TLB).

These verses set forth for us the tremendous challenge of living a life that is consistent with the doctrine we have claimed to believe. This truth is revealed over and over throughout the New Testament. A faith that does not express itself in our attitudes, our words, and our actions is not New Testament faith. James declares that "faith without works is dead" (Jas. 2:20), meaning that a faith that brings salvation is a faith that produces evidence in our lives.

A STRATEGY FOR LIFE

"But whatever happens to me, remember always to live as
Christians should, so that, whether I ever see you again or
not, I will keep on hearing good reports that you are
standing side by side with one strong purpose—to tell the
Good News fearlessly" (1:27, TLB). The words "live as
Christians should" come from a Greek word that speaks
of citizenship. Paul's readers would understand this. They
were in Philippi, a long distance from Rome, and yet were
citizens of Rome. As colonists of Rome, they were subject
to Roman law. They used the Latin language. The magistrates and leaders of their community were given Latin
titles.

There were Roman colonies all over the world, and
those colonies were literally "little Romes." The people
were governed just like those who lived in Rome. Paul is
saying in effect, "You know what it is like to be citizens
of Rome though living in Philippi. In the same way, you
are citizens of a heavenly kingdom and are bound by a
higher law than any on this earth. You are citizens of the
kingdom of God, and you are to live a life by the rules and
laws of God's kingdom."

When they approached life, they were not to be intimidated by the laws of men or to be threatened and molded
by the mores of their culture. They were to live every day
in the awareness that they were strangers and pilgrims in a
foreign land. They were citizens of the heavenly kingdom,
and their ultimate allegiance was to the kingdom of God.
If we make that our strategy for life, it will affect how we
live.

The Greek word used here traces back to a root meaning
"to balance a scale." Worth is determined by how much
weight is needed to balance the scales. If we need an ounce
of gold, we would simply put weights equaling an ounce
on one side of the scale and gold on the other. When the
scales balanced, we would have an ounce of gold. We are

to measure our lives by the heavenly standard, the Word of God, and live accordingly.

Paul tells them he wants them to live this way whether he comes to see them or not. He wasn't sure what his fate was. He was in prison, and Caesar had not yet made a judgment on his case. He planned to come to them, but even if he couldn't, they were to live according to their heavenly standard. Their Christian living did not depend on him. They belonged to God. Whether Paul was there or not was of no consequence. They were to live according to their heavenly citizenship.

One of the tragedies of our day is that we have such a strong tendency to hang on to our leaders. The saddest thing that can be said to any preacher is, "I don't know what I would do without you." If our spiritual welfare is still dependent on someone, whether counselor, pastor, mother, dad, friend, or whomever, then we are still babes in Christ and are tragically immature.

The Apostle Paul had the ability to wean his converts, to let them stand on their own feet. He encouraged them to be individuals after the likeness of Christ, not dependent upon him or any other human leader.

He declares that he wants "to keep on hearing good reports that you are standing side by side with one strong purpose" (1:27, TLB). The word translated "standing side by side" indicates a strong foothold. If we were involved in a tug-of-war on a carpeted floor, we would not have any place to "dig in." But if we were out in the yard, we could dig a hole and plant our feet in that hole to brace ourselves. We would have a good foothold. That is the word Paul uses here. "Stand fast in one spirit" (KJV). "One spirit" does not refer to the Spirit of God, but the spirit produced by the Spirit of God, a spirit of courage, stamina, victory.

So many Christians today are in full-fledged retreat. They are running and hiding from that which would give them real meaning in life. Their lives seem to melt in the face of opposition. "Retreat" should not be in the Christian's vocabulary. In the spirit of courage and power that is placed in us by the Holy Spirit we are to take our stand.

"You are standing side by side with one strong purpose —to tell the Good News fearlessly." God's Spirit draws us together. "Side by side with one strong purpose" is an athletic term meaning "striving for the goal, striving to win, striving for victory." It is a picture of a team standing shoulder to shoulder, working together to achieve the goal. That is what the church is to be. The world may quarrel, but let the church be united. Let the church move toward one goal with one mind for one purpose. We are on eternal business for the King of kings. We are citizens of a heavenly kingdom. There is no place for divisiveness and schism in the church.

Whenever God can get a church anywhere to be of one mind, he can shake a city or a nation with that church. Why do we behave like citizens of this earth? Why do we conduct our relationships and our business like those who do not know God? Let the world malign and criticize, but let the church strive together for the goal that is set before us.

One of the meanings of " . . . for the faith of the gospel" (KJV) is, "the faith produced by the gospel." "Faith cometh by hearing, and hearing by the Word of God" (Rom. 10:17). We preach the gospel, and faith is the product. We are to have one mind and one heart in proclaiming the gospel that produces this faith. That is to be the goal and direction of our lives.

A SERENITY FOR LIFE

" . . .to tell the Good News fearlessly, no matter what your enemies may do." Who are the enemies that the Philippians were not to be frightened by? Was Paul talking about the Jews who had hounded him from place to place? Probably not. He may have had some of them in mind, but this particular word was normally used to refer to pagan opposition, those of a different persuasion. In a land where there was deification of human lusts and greed, where temples were erected to idols and pagan gods, anti-Christian hostility could easily arise.

"They will see this as a sign of their downfall." When we look at our problems and the opposition and say, "Praise the Lord," it frightens our enemies. It is a sure sign they are on the way down.

The confidence God gives us cannot be given anywhere else. When we demonstrate faith, confidence, power, poise, calmness in the face of adversity, it is a sign of destruction to those who oppose us. It is God's way of saying through us that he honors our faith and our commitment. God does not want us to be frightened or intimidated. Many professing Christians are scared off by the first sign of opposition. Don't be alarmed by the enemy. The calmness and serenity that God gives us is confirmation of their coming defeat.

It is also a sure sign "that he has given you eternal life with him." When we walk into the face of tremendous obstacles and difficulties with a peace and a calmness that we cannot explain, it is a sure sign that we are saved, that we belong to God. That kind of peace only comes from God. It is a witness in our hearts that God has placed his Spirit within us.

Everyone of us who belong to the Lord have had experiences like that. Something happened and we didn't react as we thought we would. The peace that we felt at that time of confusion, the comfort we felt at that time of crisis and tragedy was inexplicable. There was no way to explain it with human logic. God did it! It is a sure sign of God's presence within us.

A SUFFERING FOR LIFE

"For to you has been given the privilege not only of trusting him but also of suffering for him. We are in this fight together. You have seen me suffer for him in the past; and I am still in the midst of a great and terrible struggle now, as you know so well" (1:29, 30, TLB). The Philippians had seen Paul suffer persecution at Philippi. They had seen him suffer for Christ's sake. Now they heard that he was suffering in prison. They saw it and heard about it, and they were experiencing the same conflict. "Fight" is an athletic term, the Greek word *agōn*. The word used to describe the agony of Jesus in the Garden of Gethsemane was *agōnea*. The word *agōn* is from the same root. It is the idea of a conflict, but not a battlefield. It refers to a sports arena, a contest. We are athletes for Christ. We are in a conflict that calls for our best, a game of life in which God has placed us. Now we will find out the quality of our character. We will have a chance to see whether we are quitters or whether we will trust God with all our heart. We are in the arena for Christ, struggling for the prize, reaching for the goal in order that there may be honor given to Christ.

"For to you has been given the privilege not only of trusting him. . . ." We all know that trusting in Christ is what saves us. But Paul continues, ". . .but also of suffering for him." He is talking specifically about the suffering that we face because we bear the name of Jesus, the pressure that comes upon us because we say, "I belong to Christ."

Simon Peter had a problem with that. Remember when Jesus was being tried and someone said, "You belong to Jesus, don't you?" "Oh, not me," Peter answered. When it came to suffering, he couldn't handle it. He denied even knowing Christ. Suffering because we belong to Jesus is what Paul is describing. What trials are there in our lives because we are Christians? At home? At school? At work?

Is there pressure being put upon us because we belong to Jesus? If there is not, there is something wrong with our witness for Christ, with the testimony we are giving. If we are not suffering the persecution that comes from belonging to Christ, then we are not standing for Christ in our lives as we should.

Genuine belief always costs something. And if we believe in Jesus Christ, it will cause us to face suffering and persecution. "For to you has been given the privilege not only of trusting him but also of suffering for him" (1:29, TLB). If we are to fulfill the purpose for which we were created, we will suffer.

We belong to a heavenly kingdom to which the world is antagonistic. The world does not understand the laws of God's kingdom. The world says, "If you strike me, I will strike you back." Jesus says, "If you strike me, I will turn the other cheek." The world says, "I am going to steal everything I can from you." Jesus says, "If you steal my shirt, I will give you my coat." The world says, "I am going to force you to do what I want you to do." Jesus says, "When you have made me go a mile, I will walk another mile with you." We are subjects of a different kingdom, and we will suffer because of the antagonism between God's kingdom and the earthly kingdom.

We not only believe in Christ, but suffer for his sake, experiencing the same agony, striving for the same goals that we see in those who went before. Paul said, "You saw this conflict in me and you hear it to be in me. I want you to be on the same team with me." We can sense that as the Philippians heard this, their spirits leaped within them. Within their hearts was the challenge and the adventure of standing with the aged warrior in a battle against the evil one. They stood with the ancient competitor, experiencing the same agony, the same pressure, reaching for the same goal, because they shared the same citizenship.

The
Fellowship
of Love
Philippians 2:1-4

"IS THERE ANY such thing as Christians cheering each other up? Do you love me enough to want to help me? Does it mean anything to you that we are brothers in the Lord, sharing the same Spirit? Are your hearts tender and sympathetic at all? Then make me truly happy by loving each other and agreeing wholeheartedly with each other, working together with one heart and mind and purpose. Don't be selfish; don't live to make a good impression on others. Be humble, thinking of others as better than yourself. Don't just think about your own affairs, but be interested in others, too, and in what they are doing" (2:1-4, TLB).

The Philippian church has as few problems as any church we find in the New Testament. In fact, there are many wonderful commendations which the Apostle Paul gives to these Christians in Philippi. But as perfect as the church was, as strong as it was, it too had some problems. There has never been a perfect church. The church is for folks just like us who have been touched by the grace of God, whose lives have been changed, whose sins have been forgiven. With a group of very ordinary people who are committed to Jesus, God does some significant and supernatural things.

As good as this church was, there existed the danger of

disharmony and disunity. They were not immune to strife or being disagreeable with each other. This is the greatest danger of every healthy church. Few of our churches fall into heresy. We are not likely to become liberal and deny certain basic tenets of the Christian faith. But wherever we have people who hold deep convictions, we have the possibility that arguing and disunity will exist.

Bear in mind that this problem was not critical in Philippi. If we desire to see how Paul dealt with the critical problem of disharmony, turn to 1 Corinthians. He dealt severely with the Corinthian Christians, but here there are no threats, no final warnings. Paul gives gentle teaching on a danger all of us face in our churches today.

A FELLOWSHIP OF HARMONY

"Is there any such thing as Christians cheering each other up?" We need always to be reminded that we have one thing in common—Jesus. We are in Christ. We are knit together in his love. That is what makes us one. Paul is pleading here for a unity that goes beyond creeds, beyond doctrine and dogma or our agreeing on a certain form of worship for the church. It is a unity "in Christ" (KJV). The first ingredient of a harmonious fellowship is "consolation [encouragement] in Christ."

The second ingredient found in this passage is love. "Do you love me enough to want to help me?" Our love for each other and our love for Christ ought to encourage us, console us, challenge us, and keep us united.

Thirdly he says, "We are . . .sharing the same Spirit." The Spirit dwelt in them and they were not their own— they were purchased with a price. Their common experience with the Spirit of God in their lives bound them together.

"Are your hearts tender and sympathetic at all?" Tenderness and sympathy are emotions produced by the Holy Spirit in us, and thus are certainly important ingredients of a harmonious church.

"Then make me truly happy by loving each other and agreeing wholeheartedly with each other, working together with one heart and mind and purpose" (2:2, TLB). This was an added incentive for a harmonious fellowship. It would greatly bless and please the heart of the great apostle if the Philippians were knit together as one.

The phrase "agreeing wholeheartedly" does not refer to intellectual understanding. It refers to an attitude with which we face life. Paul is telling them to have a common attitude toward life. That is one goal of the church—to view things from the same perspective, with the same attitude.

He admonishes them to keep "loving each other." They were to love each other with great fervency and with the same zealousness. Love has been and continues to be the distinguishing characteristic of the Christian.

"...working together with one heart and mind and purpose." Our lives, our thoughts, our intents, our attitudes, everything about us must move together. When we have this kind of harmonious fellowship, we can disagree agreeably. People of strong convictions, though they have given great consideration to the Christian life, will have disagreements. There is no way that everyone will agree on everything. What Paul is saying here is that among people with diverse ideas, who may often disagree on some concepts, there is an overriding purpose that links their lives together. Even their disagreement can enhance their progress toward that goal. As members of Christ's church, we are to build a fellowship of love, a fellowship of concern that reaches out to touch the lives of those around our communities and, indeed, around the world, with the

gospel of Jesus Christ. We must strive together to bring
them to know Christ and to teach them to know all the
things that have been entrusted to us.

A FELLOWSHIP OF DISHARMONY

Paul mentions several things that cause discord. First of
all he says, "Don't be selfish." The word translated "selfish" refers to more of a group type of selfishness than a
personal one. This was the problem in Corinth. One
group supported and followed Cephas, another Paul,
another Christ, etc. They began to argue. They had cliques
that were at each other's throats. One group was more
"spiritual" than another. Putting aside our selfishness, we
are to be one.

Another way of saying that would be, "Don't divide up
into parties. Don't divide the young against the old, the
men against the women, the black against the white, the
rich against the poor, the educated against the unedu-
cated, etc."

"Don't live to make good impressions on others," Paul
goes on. Now he gets down to an individual basis. This is
translated "vainglory" in the King James Version. The
Greek describes a man who makes great claims for himself
by putting everyone else down. No one is as spiritual as
he is. No one knows as much as he does. No one has the
prayer life he has. We are not to act like that.

"Be humble, thinking of others as better than yourself.
Don't just think about your own affairs, but be interested
in others, too, and in what they are doing." Rather than
lifting ourselves up and putting the other fellow down, we
should be just the opposite. We should look for the best
in the other person, that which we can encourage in him,
that which we can praise in him. That should be the goal
of our lives. A humble caring for others is self-forgetful-

ness, a spirit that is the opposite of arrogance and pride, an alternative to spiritual superiority. A spirit of love for the other person looks for that which is best.

It would be amazing what God could do with us if we had that kind of attitude. We must not vie against each other for position and prestige. We must not carry false humility and lift ourselves up while we put everyone else down. We need a humble spirit in the church. A harmonious fellowship is one that is anchored in Jesus Christ. We love each other because we love him. He moves in us to bring us to himself and to lead us to new spiritual discoveries, achievements, and blessings. They are ours because of what God does in us together. That is what God wants to do in the fellowship of the church.

But even a healthy church faces the danger of disharmony. If there is any area that Satan will attack, it is at the point of dividing our interests and our allegiance. He will try to fragment our direction and our purpose. We must not allow that to happen. Loving each other more intently and loving our Lord more completely each day, we better reflect the spirit of Christ, a spirit of unity and harmony, so God can use us to bless those around us and to achieve the purpose for which he has placed us here.

The results that God wants to produce come through people who are committed to each other and to the Lord with a harmony that nothing can destroy. There is no criticism that we would believe about each other. There is no gossip that could be spread that we would allow to come between us. Nothing that we encounter would destroy the harmony and unity God has produced.

Possessing the Mind of Christ
Philippians 2:5-8

PAUL NOW MAKES the highest possible appeal: the example of Jesus Christ.

"Your attitude should be the kind that was shown us by Jesus Christ, who, though he was God, did not demand and cling to his rights as God, but laid aside his mighty power and glory, taking the disguise of a slave and becoming like men. And he humbled himself even further, going so far as actually to die a criminal's death on a cross" (2:5-8, TLB).

HIS DISPOSITION

First Paul speaks of the moral temper of Jesus Christ, the characteristic of unselfishness that characterized his life. He challenged the Philippians to view life from the perspective of Jesus Christ. The attitude Jesus held toward life was one of condescension and a willingness to suffer humiliation. He came down from heaven to where we were so he could serve us and bring us to God. He stooped from heaven to earth in order that he might redeem us. If we are to have the same attitude that Jesus had, we will seek to serve rather than to be served. We will seek to minister rather than to be ministered unto.

Jesus himself spoke of this: "So Jesus called them to him and said, 'As you know, the kings and great men of the earth lord it over the people; but among you it is different. Whoever wants to be great among you must be your servant. And whoever wants to be greatest of all must be the slave of all. For even I, the Messiah, am not here to be served, but to help others, and to give my life as a ransom for many' " (Mark 10:42-45, TLB).

There is no passage anywhere in the New Testament that more clearly defines the attitude of Christ toward life than this one. He came to serve. That was his purpose. He did not come so someone could wait on him, cater to him, or minister to him. He came that he might minister to others. He introduced a new criterion of greatness: "If you would be great, you must become a servant." That is the attitude of Christ.

We must imitate that spirit. Why do we get upset? Because someone doesn't serve us. They don't cater to our ego, our whims, our ideas. We become distressed because someone does not wait on us. If our goal in life was to serve others and minister to others we would not feel that way. But as long as we selfishly say, "This is mine," "I have a right to do this," or "You have no right to demand this of me," we will have frustration and despair. We need the spirit of service which Jesus possessed. As long as we are seeking *our* comfort, we will never be a comfort to others. As long as we are seeking *our* satisfaction, we will not give satisfaction to others. The spirit of selfishness is characteristic of the carnal life. If we are to have unity in the fellowship of the church, we must have the attitude of Christ as we look at each other and the world. As we do, our desire will be to minister and to help others. Our daily prayer should be for God to give us that disposition.

THE DEITY

None of us can fully grasp what the deity of Christ means, but verse 6 helps us. Paul says first of all, "though he was

God." The idea is that he always existed, he always was God. He existed prior to his coming into the world. He existed "in the form of God" (KJV). He was, is, and shall be God.

Two Greek words were translated "form," and we don't have any English words that can fully explain them. One of the words meant, "that which is unchanging, unalterable." For instance, we are a part of the human race. We possess humanity. We can never stop possessing humanity no matter what we do. Only when God changes us when we join him in eternity will that change. Another Greek word referred to the outward form, the mask. We have changed a lot since we were born. We were only a few inches long and weighed a few pounds then. We have grown. Our outward form has changed and is changing. We experience infancy, childhood, adolescence, young manhood or womanhood, middle age, old age, etc. The outward form is constantly changing.

The Greek word *schema* described the outward form, that which changes. *Morpha* referred to the essential nature, that which doesn't change. The word that Paul uses in this passage to depict Jesus existing in the form of God is *morpha*. Christ doesn't change. He has within him the unchanging nature and character of God.

Because of this, Christ "did not demand and cling to his rights as God" (2:6, TLB). There are not two deities vying to see which is the most important. God and Jesus are not competing to see who is the most powerful. They are one and the same. Jesus is in essence and by nature God. Because of that, he did not regard equality with God a thing to which to cling. He "thought it not robbery to be equal with God" (KJV). That could mean two things. It could mean that he had already equality with God, so he didn't have to grab it or fight for it. The word translated "cling" means "to clutch" or "to snatch away." Jesus, the very essence of God, did not have to grab deity away from God. It was already his.

Or it could mean that he voluntarily laid aside his equality with God (in one sense) so he could come to earth and serve us. He didn't consider the benefits of his equality with God something to be jealously clutched to himself. So he left his place of honor and equality with God in eternity and came here to serve us. This is the best interpretation. Jesus did not consider equality with God something to be jealously clung to, but voluntarily laid aside the manifestation of his deity and his glory. He did not cease to be God, but he gave up "his rights as God."

HIS DEVOTION
Christ "laid aside his mighty power and glory, taking the disguise of a slave and becoming like men (2:7, TLB). He "made himself of no reputation" (KJV). The Greek means "to pour out until it is all gone." He emptied himself. But he did not stop being divine. Here is one of the mysteries of our faith.

A literal translation of verse 7 would be: "He emptied himself, taking the form of a bond servant." There is the word *morpha* again. Christ took upon himself the essential nature of a slave, the actual character of a servant. The humanity of Jesus was no charade. He was fully human, but also fully divine. Here is the mystery of the God-Man. Paul here declares, "Here is Jesus Christ who was the very nature, the very form, the very character of God and yet emptied himself to become the very nature, the very character of a servant." His devotion was so great that he emptied himself so he could serve us.

Can we now see how much Jesus wants to bless our lives? Can we see how much Jesus wants to minister to us? He voluntarily laid aside the *shekinah* glory that belonged only to him and clothed himself in a vesture of clay. He took upon himself "the likeness [*schema*] of men" (1:7, KJV). How much he wanted to serve and minister to us!

Paul Harvey tells a very beautiful story that illustrates this truth, a story about a man who lived on a farm in the country. It was Christmas Eve and he was warming himself by a fire, reading the paper. His family had all gone into the nearby village for Christmas Eve church services. As he was reading, he heard a loud thumping. Thinking someone was at the door, he opened it, but found no one there. About the time he got settled in his chair, he heard the thumping again. He was rather bewildered as to what was causing it until he realized that something was striking the bay window in the den. He went to the window and opened the curtain. To his amazement, a flock of birds was flying into the window. A snowstorm had blown in, and the birds had been caught away from their shelter. The warmth of the lighted window attracted the birds, and they were literally flying into that plate glass window in an effort to find warmth. They would freeze to death if they didn't soon find some shelter and provision.

The man, who had refused to go with his family to church because he had no interest in the Christ of Christmas, felt great compassion for the birds. He tried every way he could think of to get the birds to shelter and safety. He opened the barn door and turned the light on, then tried to shoo them in. But every time he got close to them, he only frightened them the more and they scurried off into the night, only to come back and pound into the window again. Then he made a trail of bread crumbs from the house to the barn, but to no avail.

"If I could just communicate with them," he thought. "If I could just tell them I don't want to hurt them. If I could just make them understand that I love them and want to help them. But I am a man and they are birds, and we don't speak the same language. If I could just commu-

nicate with them. . ." Then he thought, "If I could just
become a bird, they wouldn't be afraid of me, they would
trust me. If I could just become a bird. . ."

At that moment the bells of the church rang in the distance, sounding out the message of Christmas. The man
sank to his knees with a prayer to the Father who had
become man in the person of Jesus Christ in order to communicate his love to us, to save us from dying.

He who was perfectly God did not selfishly cling to the
privileges of deity, but voluntarily laid them down in
order to become a servant for us. What great devotion our
Lord displayed toward us!

When we feel that God doesn't care about us, we need
to realize anew what God had done to say, "I love you."
He has even put on the body of a man in order that he
might reveal his heart of love.

HIS DEATH

"And he humbled himself even further, going so far as
actually to die a criminal's death on a cross" (2:8, TLB).
Many of us have been made low, but we didn't do it ourselves. But Jesus humbled himself. His humiliation was
voluntary. No one forced him to become man. No one
forced him to die. He went obediently to the cross. His
death was the climax and the price of his humility.

The invitation of Jesus to follow him is an invitation to
humiliation and death. "Come and die," he said. That is
what it means to follow Jesus. We are to die to self, to our
ambitions and rights. The problem with many people who
claim the name of Christ is that they have not died. They
have not come to a place of crucifixion of self. They have
not come to a place of making their bodies a living sacrifice acceptable unto God. Just as Jesus humbly bowed
himself in obedience to God even though it meant suffer-

ing and death, so we, if we are to experience the kind of life that God wants us to know, must die to sin.

It is significant that in the midst of a great appeal for harmony and unity, such as we find in the first four verses, Paul points us to the example of Christ, who was equal with God and yet became obedient even to death on the cross.

We must identify with Christ and his cross in our lives. The cross has become the rallying point over the centuries for the Christian faith. It is the cross whereby God revealed his love. There Christ, while we were still sinners and enemies of his, died for us. Paul said, "For I determined not to know any thing among you, save Jesus Christ, and him crucified" (1 Cor. 2:2, KJV). It was the cross that represented God's masterstroke, his master appeal to the hearts of mankind. It was the cross that demonstrated the great lengths to which God would go to see men saved. If we are to follow Jesus, we must follow him by way of the cross. We are to die with him.

A servant or slave...death—these words offend the modern mind. But Jesus emptied himself, served, died. Let us "follow his steps" (1 Pet. 2:21, KJV).

It is not the service he renders, but the spirit in which he renders it that distinguishes the Christian. Other men may feed the poor, care for the needy, or help the illiterates of our world. The Christian may do so also. How can we tell the difference between humanitarianism and spiritual ministry? The difference is the spirit with which it is done, a spirit of humility and self-forgetfulness, a spirit that does not demand reciprocation. This is the spirit that says, "I love you whether or not you ever love me."

Christ's love for us is unconditional. He does not demand that we deserve his love, or even that we respond to it in order for him to love us. Concerning the rich young ruler who was about to go away from Jesus, Mark 10:21 says, "Jesus beholding him loved him" (KJV). It is his nature to love us, regardless of our response. "Let this mind be in you, which was also in Christ Jesus" (2:5, KJV).

We must not just minister to those we like. We must not minister out of duty. We must view life as Christ views it. Whatever we do, we do it as unto the Lord. Whether we eat, drink, or whatever, we should do it all for the glory of the Lord (1 Cor. 10:31). Our lives become vessels that contain his glory. The driving passion of our lives ought to be to please him, serve him, and honor him. So whether we are loving our families, serving through our church, doing our jobs, studying our homework, relating to our friends, whatever we are doing, let us do it in the spirit of Christ who gives and loves and is obedient all the way.

Have we been obedient even to the point of death, the death of the cross? Have we died to self? Or are we still dethroning Christ in our lives? Are we still demanding our rights and reacting to the pressures in an un-Christian way? We are to have the attitude and spirit of Christ.

We cry out, "I can't do that." That is true. None of us can do it. We cannot in ourselves have the attitude of Christ. Then what should we do? We must obey. As we are obedient, Christ will perform in us what we can never perform in ourselves.

Remember, one cannot crucify himself. We talk about crucifying self, but that is misleading. It is a matter of being obedient to Christ at every point where we know what his will is. As we serve him with complete abandonment to his purpose and will, we can reckon ourselves dead to sin, but alive to Christ (Rom. 6:11).

We were crucified with Christ. We were not there, but when he died we died because we have trusted in him and have become totally identified with him. Whatever he is, he is in us. As he humbled himself and emptied himself, so we are to empty ourselves in order for him to fill us. Then, full for his use and glory, we can achieve his purposes.

11

God's
Exalted
Son
Philippians 2:9-11

BECAUSE JESUS RENOUNCED himself and became a man, voluntarily giving up the glory that was his in heaven and becoming obedient to the death on the cross, God exalted him to his previous glory. "Yet it was because of this that God raised him up to the heights of heaven and gave him a name which is above every other name, that at the name of Jesus every knee shall bow in heaven and on earth and under the earth, and every tongue shall confess that Jesus Christ is Lord, to the glory of God the Father" (2:9-11, TLB).

These verses are absolutely staggering. It is with a sense of awe and reverence that we approach the truth contained in them.

THE EXALTATION
God has "raised him up to the heights of heaven" (2:9, TLB). "Raised to heights" is a compound word in the original language. It is also a superlative, a common tool of the Apostle Paul. This compound word means "supremacy of the highest order," the highest kind of exaltation. God has given Christ the highest possible name he could have given. Some suggest that the glory that Jesus voluntarily gave up God has now given back to him.

This concept runs throughout the New Testament. Jesus himself said, "For everyone who tries to honor himself shall be humbled; and he who humbles himself shall be honored" (Luke 14:11, TLB). God always rewards the humble, but resists the proud. This is a principle of life. Those who determine to go through life arrogantly, demanding their rights, will find themselves humiliated. Those who humble themselves before God will find themselves exalted.

The best example of this is Jesus Christ. He is the greatest possible example of the kind of spirit we ought to have in this life. Jesus humbled himself, emptied himself, literally poured out himself for us. As a result, God has given him supreme exaltation.

God "gave him a name which is above every other name" (2:9, TLB). "Gave" can be translated "bestowed." This usually refers to the gracious gift of salvation by God to us, but here he bestowed something *on Christ*. What did he bestow? A name which is above every name. Most major translations rightly translate this "*the* name."

There are many different ideas about the name that was bestowed on Christ. Some say that the name merely represented his character. In the Old Testament the name of God was sometimes used synonymously with his presence. Others say that what God has given to Jesus is not just a name by which he can be called, but a wonderful dignity, honor, and supremacy. This ties in with the fact that the definite article "the" is before "name." God has given him "*the* name."

Jehovah God says, "I have sworn by myself and I will never go back on my word, for it is true—that every knee in all the world shall bow to me, and every tongue shall swear allegiance to my name" (Isa. 45:23, TLB). This verse in Philippians is almost a direct quote from Isaiah. Since this is what Paul declares has been given to Jesus Christ, it is obvious that "the name above every name" is this—

Jehovah God. As further confirmation, the word "Lord" (1:11) in the New Testament is the equivalent of the word "Jehovah" in the Old Testament. Jesus is called Jehovah God. Jehovah God is the God-Man.

Some might ask, "Wasn't he already God? Why does God have to give him the name if he has always been God?" When Jesus was resurrected from the earth, he went back to heaven with a body. Before, he had been the Son of God without human form. When he went back to glory, he went not as the Son a spirit, but he went back with a body. For the first time a man, a God-Man, bore *the* name. Jesus Christ bears *the* name Lord Jehovah, which is above every name.

THE ADORATION

Paul goes on, "...that at the name of Jesus every knee shall bow in heaven and on earth and under the earth, and every tongue shall confess that Jesus Christ is Lord" (2:10, 11a, TLB). At this name which God has given to Jesus, every knee bows. Bowing the knee calls for a commitment of the will, which is an expression of the mind, so Paul must be speaking of the intelligent universe. At the name Jesus, every intelligent being will bow. Everyone is going to give homage, respect, and worship to Jesus Christ. The entire, intelligent, created universe will bow before him. What a tremendous thought that is!

What a tremendous time that will be when every knee will bow and every tongue will confess that Jesus Christ is Lord. What a great tragedy it must be in the heart of God to see so much rebellion to God and so much resistance to his purposes now. Such rebellion is all futile, because one day every knee will bow before Jesus Christ.

"Lord" is a word of superlative emphasis itself. It means owner. He is the owner of all of the created universe.

"Lord" is a word of great proportions; yet we casually toss it about. We use it as though we were talking about popcorn or peanuts, as though we were speaking of things of no consequence at all. We talk glibly about Jesus as Lord. We put it on bumper stickers and plaques on the wall. I am not against such uses of the word, but somehow our familiarity with the term has caused us to lose sight of its meaning and importance. No man can say that Jesus is Lord except by the Holy Spirit. We are not talking about just saying a word, but about experiencing its fullness.

Remember when Mary went to the garden to look for the body of Jesus and could not find him? She was apparently crying when someone approached her. Through her tears she thought it was the gardener. She asked, "Where have you taken him?" When Jesus spoke her name, she said, "Lord, Lord." It was not just a name, not just four letters put together in the alphabet in a certain order, not just a particular title. It was an expression of deep love and commitment.

When we say "Lord," we are saying, "Jesus, you are my Master. I will do anything you tell me to do. I am taking my hands off my life; it is yours. I belong to you and I am going to follow you." There is much glib lip service given to that name today, but to call Jesus Lord is the most difficult thing, humanly speaking, that we can do. To call him Lord means to deny ourselves, to turn loose of our own strength and sufficiency and obey him without question. We do not like that! We want to know his will so we can think about it a while. But to call him "Lord" means that we follow him without question. If he is truly our "Lord," it will make a difference in the way we live.

This passage, speaking of everyone worshiping and adoring Jesus, follows immediately after a passage dealing with his death on the cross. Why do we call Jesus Lord? Because he died for us. No one has loved us like Jesus has loved us. No one has given himself to us like Jesus gave himself to us. We do not call him Lord because we are afraid or because we stand in abject fear of him. We call him Lord because his love has invaded our lives. We love him because he first loved us.

THE APPROBATION

God exalted Jesus and bestowed upon him a name that all will worship "to the glory of God the Father" (2:11b, TLB). The whole purpose of the life of Jesus was to give honor to God, to bring praise and glory to him. When the Savior was sacrificed on the cross, it was to bring glory to God. When God raised him up, it was to bring glory to God. When God gave him that exalted name of eminent supremacy, it was to bring glory to God. Everything about the life of Jesus brought glory to God.

This passage is not here to create some artificial civil war among the Godhead. Not at all. Jesus and God are equal. But Jesus did everything he did in order to give glory to God. This is here to tell us why we ought to do what we do. Every breath we draw ought to be for God's glory.

That is the real way to be happy. Jesus was supremely happy giving glory to God. He loved every moment of it. That is what his heart longed to do. Not for a moment did he regret the pain and agony of the cross. While it was torturous to endure, it brought God glory and Jesus rejoiced in giving glory to God. Everything about our lives ought to give glory to God too. When we can look at life as being an opportunity to bring glory to God, it will revolutionize and brighten the whole horizon of our lives. It will change everything we do, every relationship we have, every attitude we hold, because we will view every moment of life as an opportunity to give honor to God.

12 Work Out Your Own Salvation
Philippians 2:12, 13

"DEAREST FRIENDS, when I was there with you, you were always so careful to follow my instructions. And now that I am away you must be even more careful to do the good things that result from being saved, obeying God with deep reverence, shrinking back from all that might displease him. For God is at work within you, helping you want to obey him, and then helping you do what he wants" (2:12, 13, TLB).

PERSONAL INDEPENDENCE
In these two verses, Paul takes a look at two sides of a coin. In verse 12 he talks about personal independence and in verse 13 he talks about personal dependence. In verse 12 he tells them, "Keep on obeying Christ and living the way you ought to live, even though I am not there. Do not be dependent upon someone else's strength. You have given your life to Christ, you belong to him, now stand tall. Work out your own salvation." The emphasis is on their own personal faith. They were to stand in obedience to Christ, regardless of Paul's presence or absence.

This matter of personal independence is one of the most difficult principles to learn. It is one thing for us to be

Christian in deportment when we are in church, surrounded by people who feel the same way, but it is another thing to be Christian outside the church. Paul
realized the tremendous pressure brought to bear upon
the Philippians and he realized how much his presence
encouraged them. This is true of us also. We may have a
problem with our temper or controlling our language, etc.,
but when we are around certain people whom we respect
greatly as Christians, we have everything in control. They
strengthen us. We draw upon them. But when we get
away from their strength and encouragement, we falter.

Paul is telling us in this passage that we need to move
beyond dependence on someone else's strength, drawing
upon someone else's commitment. We must stand for
ourselves, commit our lives to Jesus and be obedient to
him for ourselves. It is immaterial whether or not anyone
else stands up for Christ. We must stand up for him. God
wants us to stand in our own strength and not be intimidated by anyone. It is important for us to be obedient
when our fellow Christians are watching, but it is also
important to be obedient when no one is watching.

The word translated "salvation" (2:12, KJV) is used
many different ways in the Bible. It sometimes refers to
the entire process of salvation, which biblically has three
phases. The initial experience of salvation is forgiveness
of sin. Sometimes the word "salvation" in the New
Testament speaks only of that phase. There is also the concept of being saved from the power of sin as we grow,
mature, and gain spiritual victory in our lives. At other
times the word salvation is used to speak of final deliverance, the end of the age when we stand before the Lord.
That does not mean we have to hold out to the end in order
to be saved. That is simply the final stage of salvation, the
final deliverance.

In this passage, the word "salvation" refers to that

second phase. Paul is telling saved people that they are to work out what is already in their lives. He does not say "work *for* your salvation." He says, "Work *out* your salvation" (KJV). Now that we have received God's eternal life through Jesus Christ, there is so much more for us to discover. We are to grow and mature. We are to bring it to its conclusion.

The word translated "work" (KJV) means "to carry something out to its logical conclusion." A graphic illustration is the development of a human being. When we are born, we are born with everything we need to live, but we have to learn how to use what we have. We are born with legs, but we have to learn how to use them. We are born with a brain that is capable of vast knowledge, but we must learn how to use it. Most of the frustration we face is the frustration of learning to use what we have. This is the process of growing up, of maturing. The same thing is true spiritually. We begin in a relationship with the Lord and we are to work at letting it reach its conclusion. There are victories to be claimed and virtues to be developed, and this is the working out of our salvation.

The phrase "with deep reverence, shrinking back" (TLB) is translated "fear and trembling" in the King James Version. However, it does not mean "terror," but "submission" and "reverence to God." It means not to be flippant about it. A lot of folks are very cocky about their salvation. They are very self-sufficient about it. We are to carry salvation to its ultimate conclusion, and we are to do it in deep submission to God and with awe and reverence of him.

If we love someone, we are not afraid of what they might do to us, but of what we might do to them. We are not to be afraid of what God will do to us, but we should be afraid that we may bring shame and embarrassment to him.

PERSONAL DEPENDENCE

Paul also talks about human responsibility. The idea of being "careful to do the good things that result from being saved" (2:12, TLB) implies freedom, responsibility, and ability to do it. In verse 13 Paul continues, "For God is at work within you, helping you want to obey him, and then helping you do what he wants." We have seen personal independence, and now we have personal dependence. We have to work out our own salvation, but God is the one working through us. On one hand we have human responsibility, and on the other divine sovereignty. They are spoken of together without apology.

We need not feel that we have to explain that every time we come to it. God's Word teaches both the free will of man and the sovereignty of God. Though we cannot comprehend this, in God's mind and wisdom the two are not contradictory. God never withholds his salvation from man, but man may refuse God's salvation. That is the incomparable paradox of the New Testament. At one moment Paul says we are to work out our salvation with fear and trembling. Then he turns right around and declares that it is God who is at work within us to do it.

The word "work" in the thirteenth verse is the Greek word from which we get our word "energy." It is God who is energizing us, causing us to serve him. We are to serve God with all our strength and when we do, we discover God was doing it in us all the time. We are to let God work in us. We see this over and over again in the New Testament. Jesus said, "My Father worketh hitherto, and I work" (John 5:17, KJV). That is a good example of this concept. God was at work and Jesus was at work. Jesus, talking about the blind man who was healed, said, "Neither hath this man sinned, nor his parents: but that the works of God should be made manifest in him. I must work the works of him that sent me, while it is day; the night cometh, when no man can work" (John 9:3, 4, KJV).

There is the same idea: man's work, God's work.

The Christian life and maturity is at one and the same time the work of God and the work of man. "For it is God which worketh in you both to will and to do of his good pleasure" (2:13, KJV). "Will" is a word that means "to desire something as a result of emotion and not reason." God's Holy Spirit is within us, charging us up, energizing us. As a result, there is a desire for us to let God do his work. Very simply, if we do not desire to do the work of God, we have not allowed the Spirit of God to move in us. God is at work in us to cause us to will and to do what he wants us to do. We depend on him.

We are independent of each other in the sense that in whatever circumstances we find ourselves, we are to stand firm—alone if need be. But at the same time, we are each dependent. God, through the Holy Spirit, prompts our impulses, thoughts, intents, actions. If we do not have the right thoughts and impulses, if we are not obedient, it is because we have refused the Lord a place in our lives. When he has free rein in us, he works in us to cause us to desire and to do what is his will and his purpose.

"IN EVERYTHING you do, stay away from complaining and arguing, so that no one can speak a word of blame against you. You are to live clean, innocent lives as children of God in a dark world full of people who are crooked and stubborn. Shine out among them like beacon lights, holding out to them the Word of Life. Then when Christ returns how glad I will be that my work among you was so worthwhile. And if my lifeblood is, so to speak, to be poured out over your faith which I am offering up to God as a sacrifice—that is, if I am to die for you—even then I will be glad, and will share my joy with each of you. For you should be happy about this, too, and rejoice with me for having this privilege of dying for you" (2:14-18, TLB).

Apparently the Philippian church was a dynamic, exemplary one. The only real criticism that we have seen is that there seemed to be a few ripples of dissension, a small fracture in their fellowship that appeared periodically. Paul confronts this issue by saying, "In everything you do, stay away from complaining and arguing" (2:14, TLB). Remember that in the previous passage he dealt with the matter of allowing their salvation to express itself in their lives. So we can assume that disputings and murmurings have no part in a Christian's life.

Notice the apostle says, "in everything you do." Christianity is not just a way of coming to church, praying, or giving thanks to God; it is a way of life. The pattern of our lives must not include grumbling or disputing.

The word translated "complaining" gives a picture of mumbling so words cannot be distinguished. It is the low, muffled noise that comes from a large crowd before a service begins. It is not loud dissent, but almost silent mumbling. The complaining mentioned here is a grumbling about man, not about God. It is a general grumbling about each other. "Arguing" means "to debate." Paul warns that if we don't stop grumbling, if we don't stop what is under the surface, it will become open dissension and debate. We must not be party to such a spirit.

As we read carefully through the Word of God, we discover that one of the major things God constantly warns us about is dissension. The writer of Proverbs wrote, "These six doth the Lord hate: yea, seven are an abomination unto him" (Prov. 6:16, KJV). The last thing he lists is, "he that soweth discord among brethren" (Prov. 6:19, KJV).

THE CONDUCT

As God continues to work out and express the faith that we have, there is a certain conduct that will characterize our lives. " . . .so that no one can speak a word of blame against you. You are to live clean, innocent lives as children of God" (2:15, TLB). The Greek construction shows that they were not there yet. They were not then living clean and innocent lives. Paul was saying, "If you will do everything without complaining and arguing, you will become what you ought to be." "Clean" means someone that cannot be accused. God is constantly calling us, as his children, to be above question. That is why Jesus told us to give our shirts also to one who takes our coat, or turn the other cheek if someone slaps us. It is better to be taken advantage of than to be accused. We are to be above reproach.

"Innocent" means unmixed, unadulterated. It was used in the Greek language to refer to pure wine, without any mixture of water in it. When it refers to us as human beings, it describes unmixed living, unmixed motives. Some appear to be spiritual in order to achieve a certain goal. We, as Christ's children, are to conduct ourselves so that we are above censure, so no accusation can be raised against us. We must have unmixed lives that are not filled with compromise. There must be no question about our motives or actions.

THE CONTRAST

The Philippians were to prove themselves clean and innocent children of God "in a dark world full of people who are crooked and stubborn. Shine out among them like beacon lights" (2:15, TLB). God never intended for our Christian lives to be withdrawn from the world. In the midst of the world, in the midst of wickedness, in the midst of an evil generation, we are to stand out for Christ. Our lives are to be a contrast to the world. In the midst of those who have no time for God, we are to rise as lights in a darkened sky.

We sometimes have the idea that we can be closer to God out in nature, perhaps on lonely mountains or in the wide open spaces. But the purpose of God is not for us to be withdrawn into solitary places or to get away from people. As we work out our salvation, it is to be expressed through us for one reason: so that people who are crooked and perverse, those who deliberately turn away from the truth can see the contrast. We are to appear as lights to the world.

The Greek word for "shine" does not emphasize the light that comes from the shining, but the fact that it appears. In the midst of a world whose conscience has turned to blackness, we are to rise like the moon on a dark night and cast light in the midst of the darkness. Our salvation is to be worked out through us in the midst of a crooked and perverse generation in order that God may be seen and honored.

A tragedy of our times is that most professing Christians do not live much differently than non-Christians. They look the same, talk the same, do the same things. Everything is the same except that the professing Christian goes to church. Perhaps the greatest tool Satan uses is professing Christians whose lives deny their profession.

THE CONQUEST

The Christian life is to be a conquering and victorious life. "Holding out to them the Word of Life" (2:16, TLB) means to present the gospel expecting them to take it. Here is a direct urging on the part of the Apostle Paul for these Christians to be active in sharing the gospel. No genuine Christian should be silent with the gospel. Sadly, many professing Christians witness negatively because their lives don't demonstrate the gospel. They are saying to every unsaved person, "There is nothing real about the gospel. It has not made a difference in my life."

We often think that some Christians do not witness, but they all do witness! The trouble is, some give the wrong kind of witness. They give a witness that says, "God is insignificant and unimportant in my life." As God's salvation is worked out through us, we will offer the Word of Life to those around us, expecting them to take it.

As we present the Word of Life some will receive it, so that when Jesus comes back for his saints we will be able to say that we did not waste our lives, we did not work in vain (2:16). The Apostle Paul wanted these Philippians to so live that in the day of Christ Paul could be proud of them. They would be proof that he had not wasted his life.

While this may appear selfish to some, it certainly is not, because in the next sentence Paul says that he is willing to die for them. He is about to say, "I am already being offered. My life is already being poured out. But it is all right because you are the kind of people you are." Wouldn't it be tragic to give our lives to something only to find out in the end it was all for nothing? No one wants to live and die for nothing. The Apostle Paul did not want to come to the day of Christ only to realize that he had worked in vain.

There is much more to the Christian life than just saying "yes" to Jesus and receiving eternal life. Salvation must express itself and reveal a growing and maturing relationship with the Lord. Someday we will be proud of all the labor we have bestowed, and that is not a selfish pride but a sense of honor and glory to God.

THE CONSUMMATION

"And if my lifeblood is, so to speak, to be poured out over your faith which I am offering up to God as a sacrifice—that is, if I am to die for you—even then I will be glad, and will share my joy with each of you. For you should be happy about this, too, and rejoice with me for having this privilege of dying for you" (2:17, 18, TLB). Paul draws upon the picture of an Old Testament sacrifice where an animal is placed upon the altar. Many times a drink offering would be poured across the sacrifice that was already on the altar. He is talking about an offering upon an offering. Their service and their faith was an offering to God, and now his life was being added to their sacrifice.

But they were not to mourn at the prospects of his death; they were to rejoice with him. "For me to live is Christ," he had said, "and to die is gain" (1:21, KJV). His life was unaffected by any circumstance, even death, and he was rejoicing. He wanted them to share his joy. That is the consummation of the salvation God has planted in our hearts. He forgives us of our sins, but there is more than that. That which he plants in our hearts has to express itself; it has to work its way out.

14

Partners
in the Faith
Philippians 2:19-24

"IF THE LORD is willing, I will send Timothy to see you soon. Then when he comes back he can cheer me up by telling me all about you and how you are getting along. There is no one like Timothy for having a real interest in you; everyone else seems to be worrying about his own plans and not those of Jesus Christ. But you know Timothy. He has been just like a son to me in helping me preach the Good News. I hope to send him to you just as soon as I find out what is going to happen to me here. And I am trusting the Lord that soon I myself may come to see you" (2:19-24, TLB).

Recognizing that talk of his impending martyrdom would cast a shadow of despair upon his readers, Paul immediately sets out to lift their spirits and assure them that everything is going to be all right.

Hope for the Apostle Paul was not empty expectation, an idle fond dream that he cherished in his heart. His hope was based in Jesus Christ. "But I trust in the Lord Jesus . . ." (2:19, KJV). Jesus Christ was Paul's Lord, his life. So of course his hope, his trust for the future was wrapped up in Jesus Christ. Paul's plans centered in Jesus Christ. So should ours.

Timothy was an outstanding young man. He was in all likelihood Paul's closest friend, his most trusted companion. We know he came either from Derbe or Lystra. His mother was named Eunice and his grandmother Lois. His mother was a Jew and his father a Greek. We know that Timothy himself was uncircumcised, which indicates he was not trained in the customs and traditions of Judaism. We know that he was converted some time during the first two missionary journeys of the Apostle Paul. He bursts on the scene during the second missionary journey.

Paul saw tremendous potential in young Timothy. He saw a young man he could trust and train, and he poured out his life into that young man. Timothy represented Paul in many places, often carrying messages for the great apostle. Paul believed in young Timothy and trusted him so completely that when he desired a message to be delivered of needed information that would be absolutely reliable, he sent Timothy. And when Timothy delivered the message, the people heard it as though Paul himself were speaking.

RECIPROCATION

Reciprocation is a part of our fellowship together. Giving and receiving is the very nature of Christian fellowship and Christian compassion. This is subtly expressed in verse 19: "If the Lord is willing, I will send Timothy to see you soon. Then when he comes back he can cheer me up by telling me all about you and how you are getting along" (TLB). The Philippians would be encouraged when they learned of his condition, but he also would be encouraged when he learned of their condition. There was a reciprocation of concern and compassion. Though he was the one in prison and the one probably facing imminent death, he was more concerned for them than he was for himself. When our fellowship and concern for each other reaches that proportion, God will move in mighty ways in our fellowship.

We have instant communication today. We can talk to anyone almost anywhere in just a few minutes. We never have to wonder very long about anybody. But the Apostle Paul was separated by many miles and many months from these Christians that he loved. Can we imagine the anticipation he builds up and how encouraged and relieved he would be when the good news came? And, from the other side, here was a church with tremendous love for the Apostle Paul. They were concerned for him. They sent money to him. They sent representatives to help him and assist him. Can we imagine how they felt after many weeks, maybe months, of hearing nothing and then they get a message? We communicate so quickly and freely that we lose something of the anticipation and the joy of the news we receive.

ISOLATION

Verses 20, 21 are sad verses. "There is no one like Timothy for having a real interest in you; everyone else seems to be worrying about his own plans and not those of Jesus Christ" (2:20, 21, TLB). In casually reading through this passage, these two verses come as a surprise. Paul speaks fondly and with love of Timothy, Epaphroditus, and others. But he also says, "There is no one else here."

The first question that comes to mind is, Where were the rest of them? Where was Luke, Onesimus, Tychicus, John Mark, Epaphras? Where were these men who had stood by him and encouraged his heart? The most logical answer seems to be that either they had not yet arrived in the city, or they had been sent on errands themselves. Certainly he is not saying that Timothy is the only one who loves them or cares for them. But apparently there was no one else available to bring Paul's message to them.

The Christians who were there were too self-centered,

too involved in their own lives and interests to have any genuine concern. Perhaps they did not know the Christians in Philippi and they were not interested in finding out about them. They were wrapped up in selfish pursuits. There was no one who loved them like Timothy did, no one who had the same concern for them. He was isolated from those who really cared. The Greek for "real interest" describes the opposite of counterfeit. Timothy's love for the brethren was for real.

"Everyone else seems to be worrying about his own plans and not those of Jesus Christ." "Everyone else" is a strong reference to the Christians where Paul was. We do not know all the implications for the Christians of whom he spoke, but we do know that this verse is all too often a description of many Christians today. Most people in church on Sunday morning are people of whom you can say, "They all seek after their own interests, not those of Christ Jesus." Their lives do not revolve around Jesus. Their energies are not given to spread his gospel. They are so concerned for their own interests and concerns that they are not concerned for the things of Jesus Christ.

Do we genuinely seek the things of Christ Jesus? Wherever we are, whatever we are doing, do we genuinely seek that which will bring honor to Christ? That is a disturbing question, but it is one that needs to be placed upon our hearts often.

PARTICIPATION

"But you know Timothy. He has been just like a son to me in helping me preach the Good News" (2:22, TLB). The word "know" means "to know from personal experience." The Philippians knew firsthand of the interest Timothy had for them. They knew from their own experience that he had proven himself to be a true and valuable messenger and associate. Notice that Paul did not say that Timothy served him, even though he did. Rather, he lifts Timothy to a level of total partnership, of complete participation in the ministry of the gospel. He was "like a son . . .in helping me." They served together and with equal responsibility. Their united purpose, their desire to honor God caused the gospel to have great progress through their ministry.

Wherever God's people are united together, lifting each other up and seeking to serve God and bring honor to him, there is always progress in the gospel. The participation of Timothy with Paul in a united and concerted effort caused the gospel to advance. Timothy was faithful, just the way a son loves to be with his dad and serve him. He participated in Paul's ministry of the gospel.

ANTICIPATION

"I hope to send him to you just as soon as I find out what is going to happen to me here" (2:23, TLB). The words "find out" mean "to turn your attention from one thing to another." Paul was concerned for those he loved and had led to Christ. He will look into his own situation, but for their sake, not his own, so he can send good news back to them. He had to wait and see what would happen with his situation. His trial would have to go before Nero, and there was no one more unpredictable than Nero. He could be released or be killed. But he was turning his attention to his own needs only so he could send word to his Philippian friends.

"And I am trusting the Lord that soon I myself may come to see you" (2:24, TLB). The beautiful conclusion of this passage is seen in the word "trusting." This is not the usual Greek word for "trust." This particular word means "to be persuaded." Paul is saying that he is persuaded in the Lord, he has a settled conviction that God is still in control. The word is in the perfect tense, which indicates he has a conviction that is completely settled, completely grounded. He has complete confidence in God. He was in prison and would be tried before one of the most cruel emperors the world had ever known. Yet he was sure that God was in control. If he were released, God would have to release him. If he were not set free, he would just simply take his sojourn in a land where there are no shadows or darkness. God is in control! No wonder he could write so many times in this little book, "Rejoice, rejoice, rejoice."

The great message of the Apostle Paul in this book is strongly expressed in this passage. Here is his utter trust in the power of God to achieve his will.

15

Loving Concern for a Brother
Philippians 2:25-30

"MEANWHILE, I thought I ought to send Epaphroditus back to you. You sent him to help me in my need; well, he and I have been real brothers, working and battling side by side. Now I am sending him home again, for he has been homesick for all of you and upset because you heard that he was ill. And he surely was; in fact, he almost died. But God had mercy on him, and on me too, not allowing me to have this sorrow on top of everything else. So I am all the more anxious to get him back to you again, for I know how thankful you will be to see him, and that will make me happy and lighten all my cares. Welcome him in the Lord with great joy, and show your appreciation, for he risked his life for the work of Christ and was at the point of death while trying to do for me the things you couldn't do because you were far away" (2:25-30, TLB).

This passage speaks of fellowship, love, and great concern for others. It speaks of reaching outside of ourselves by being concerned for others who have difficulties. This is a very beautiful passage that deals with the kind of spirit and unity that ought to be seen in God's people.

PARTNERSHIP
This spirit and unity is seen in the relationship of Paul and Epaphroditus, partners in God's work. Paul calls him a

"brother," a word that speaks of being from the same source. We who are born again spring from the same source, Jesus Christ.

Paul also says they were "battling side by side," indicating conflict with the enemies of Christ. They were fellow soldiers. Epaphroditus is seen as a man of courage, zeal, and dedication. He and Paul were in the same ministry together. From Paul's perspective, Epaphroditus was his brother in the faith, his fellow-worker in preaching the gospel, and his fellow soldier in the conflict with the enemy.

Paul recognizes that Epaphroditus had a partnership with the Philippians also. He was their messenger and their minister to Paul. Paul now declares that he was sending him back to them. The word translated "ministered" (2:25, KJV) referred to a man who had property, saw a need in the community, and at his own expense provided for that need. He may have ministered by defending his community or helping the needy. But at any rate he used his own possessions to provide for a need that would not have been met otherwise. That is how the word was used in secular society.

When it was brought into the New Testament, it was used to refer to one who served in the gospel. It was used for priestly service, for one who ministers the things of God. Epaphroditus was the Philippians' "messenger" (literally, "apostle") to Paul. But more than that, he was a priest, serving Paul and ministering to his needs.

"Now I am sending him home again, for he has been homesick for all of you and upset because you heard that he was ill" (2:26, TLB). After arriving in Rome, Epaphroditus had become deathly ill. Word had filtered back to Philippi that Epaphroditus was at the point of death. They were naturally very concerned. Epaphroditus was homesick, and this homesickness was aggravated by the fact that the Philippians knew he was sick. He did not want their peace of mind and heart marred with worry, and he wanted to see them. These Christians had a tender comradeship and fellowship in Jesus Christ.

Every one of us knows what it is like to be homesick, to want to see someone. Epaphroditus deeply wanted to return to his friends, but they had sent him to Rome to minister to Paul. If he went home, they might accuse him to quitting and not fulfilling his job. They might think he ran out on Paul. We can see something of the mixed emotions he must have felt. He wanted to go home, but he wanted to stay with Paul. He wanted to fulfill his mission, and yet he wanted to go home. In both cases his primary motive was love.

PROVISION

" . . .you heard that he was ill. And he surely was; in fact, he almost died. But God had mercy on him, and on me too, not allowing me to have this sorrow on top of everything else" (2:27, TLB). Epaphroditus had been sick, but God had mercy on him. God had provided healing for his body. Not only did God have mercy on Epaphroditus, but on Paul also. If Epaphroditus had not been healed, Paul would have borne a burden of grief.

The Apostle Paul experienced many kinds of sorrow. In 1:17 he told about enemies who were preaching Christ from envy and strife, hoping to cause him distress. What a sadness it is when two people preach the same Christ but condemn each other. Another sorrow was that he was separated from the Philippians whom he loved, friends who stood by him perhaps more than any others. If Epaphroditus had died, another sorrow would have been added to all the others.

Whatever we face in life, God will provide for our needs. That really is the message of this passage. Whatever may come our way, God will take care of us. God's mercy prevents further sadness. He has promised that nothing will come our way that he will not give us the grace and the strength to bear. "I will say this: because these experiences I had were so tremendous, God was afraid I might be puffed up by them; so I was given a physical condition which has been a thorn in my flesh, a messenger from Satan to hurt and bother me, and prick my pride. Three different times I begged God to make me well again. Each time he said, 'No. But I am with you; that is all you need. My power shows up best in weak people.' Now I am glad to boast about how weak I am; I am glad to be a living demonstration of Christ's power, instead of showing off my own power and abilities" (2 Cor. 12:7-9, TLB).

PASSION

"So I am all the more anxious to get him back to you again, for I know how thankful you will be to see him, and that will make me happy and lighten all my cares. Welcome him in the Lord with great joy, and show your appreciation, for he risked his life for the work of Christ and was at the point of death while trying to do for me the things you couldn't do because you were far away" (2:28-30, TLB). Can we imagine a man who may be executed by a cruel emperor being concerned for someone else? We would think he would be concerned about what was going to happen to him. Paul had no idea what the wicked heart of Nero would do to him. His life was in danger, and yet he was concerned for Epaphroditus and the Philippians. He sent Epaphroditus back home, so the Philippians could rejoice.

The apostle was concerned how the Philippians would receive Epaphroditus, for he told them to "show your appreciation." He did not want them to think less of their messenger because he returned home. He did not want them to think that he was a quitter. So he laid a foundation for a hero's welcome, though he himself would perhaps die at the whim of a wicked emperor.

Paul knew he would miss Epaphroditus, but it gave him a great lift to know that the Philippians would receive Epaphroditus with rejoicing. The fact that they would be joined together in fellowship and sweet harmony made Paul happy and lightened his cares (2:28). What a tremendous touch of character we see in the Apostle Paul!

"Welcome him in the Lord with great joy" (2:29, TLB). The only way we can have harmony is to receive each other in the Lord. If we receive each other in our own ideas or our own personalities, we won't be able to accept everyone. There are some folks we just don't like and who don't like us. We only have joy in all that we share together in the Lord. Here is a tremendous formula for harmony in the church: "Welcome him in the Lord with great joy, and show your appreciation."

Paul was never so immersed in his own troubles that he could forget the troubles of others. We all have problems, but we need to be sensitive to the needs of others no matter what we face. Even though Paul was close to death, he was concerned about how the Philippians would receive Epaphroditus.

"For he risked his life for the work of Christ and was at the point of death while trying to do for me the things you couldn't do because you were far away" (2:30, TLB). The word translated "risked" was a gambling word referring to rolling the dice. How was Epaphroditus gambling his life? In the Roman Empire if one showed sympathy to a prisoner, he could be forced to bear the same sentence the prisoner bore. If one visited a prisoner, he ran the risk of being tossed in jail himself. But a group in the early church, called "the gamblers," risked their lives visiting prisoners and caring for the sick. Epaphroditus was gambling his life for Jesus' sake. Christians ought to be a people of reckless courage! We ought to be willing to risk all for Christ.

Epaphroditus was willing to risk his life "to do the things you couldn't do because you were far away." Paul was not intimating that the Philippians had failed him and that Epaphroditus was doing what they had failed to do. He was saying that Epaphroditus stood where they couldn't stand. He filled a gap they couldn't fill. They couldn't come, but he was willing to risk his life to represent them and stand in their place.

We see something of the tremendous unity of purpose that drove the early church. It is no wonder that it turned an empire on its ear. It is no wonder that it changed the course of the world and set the pace for Christianity down through the years. These early Christians were a people of a single purpose, heart, and mind, and they moved together in a partnership and with a passion for each other that absolutely shook the world. If we could somehow recapture that spirit, God would again shake the world through his people.

Inadequate
Resources
Philippians 3:1-7

16

WE NEED TO REMEMBER that the Apostle Paul was at one time Saul of Tarsus, the chief tormentor and persecutor of the church. In fact, the conversion of Saul of Tarsus is one of the best proofs of the resurrection of Jesus Christ. How else can we explain such a radical transformation of character? Saul of Tarsus was a hate-filled, power-driven man who was determined to erase the name of Jesus Christ from the earth. Yet he became the foremost proponent of the Christian faith. When we read his pedigree in this passage, we realize how far he came. Once the great leader among the Pharisees and an opponent of Christ, he became a great missionary and preacher.

"Whatever happens, dear friends, be glad in the Lord. I never get tired of telling you this and it is good for you to hear it again and again. Watch out for those wicked men —dangerous dogs, I call them—who say you must be circumcised to be saved. For it isn't the cutting of our bodies that makes us children of God; it is worshiping him with our spirits. That is the only true 'circumcision.' We Christians glory in what Christ Jesus has done for us and realize that we are helpless to save ourselves. Yet if anyone ever had reason to hope that he could save himself, it would be I. If others could be saved by what they are, certainly I could! For I went through the Jewish initiation ceremony when I was eight days old, having been born into a pure-blooded Jewish home that was a branch of the old original Benjamin family. So I was a real Jew if there ever was one! What's more, I was a member of the Pharisees who demand the strictest obedience to every Jewish law and custom. And sincere? Yes, so much so that I greatly persecuted the church; and I tried to obey every Jewish rule and regulation right down to the very last point. But all these things that I once thought very worthwhile—now I've thrown them all away so that I can put my trust and hope in Christ alone" (3:1-7, TLB).

THE REPETITION USED

The repetition Paul used is one of the most important aspects of this passage. "Whatever happens, dear friends, be glad in the Lord. I never get tired of telling you this and it is good for you to hear it again and again" (3:1, TLB). In the first part of this verse, Paul tells us to "be glad in the Lord," and to never stop being glad. Our rejoicing is in the Lord. There is no joy in anything else.

The Christian life of joy is an unfolding quest, an increasing delight. Our joy in Christ keeps growing and maturing. Many people get saved, but never mature, never enlarge their vision, never grow in their relationship with the Lord. In this passage, we are told to keep on rejoicing, never to tire of it. Our faith is a holy quest, a wonderful spiritual adventure of pursuing the joy of Christ. "Every day with Jesus is sweeter than the day before."

We have already mentioned that the key word in the book of Philippians is "joy," and Paul comments on the fact that he is repeating that theme in this passage. He says, "I never get tired of telling you this and it is good for you to hear it again and again." There is a need for repetition in the Christian faith. Many times we hear something preached or taught that we have heard before, and we will hear it again, because the basics of Christianity can never be overemphasized. We may have heard them today or yesterday, but we need to hear them again tomorrow.

One of the errors of our day is our overemphasis on finding new ways to proclaim the gospel. There is nothing wrong in trying to be creative in presenting the gospel, but sometimes we get carried away and forget to preach it clearly or at all. Paul says that we cannot hear the basics too much. When we read and study the Bible, we find the same recurring themes throughout the Word of God: man's inadequacy, God's sufficiency, man's rebellion, God's grace and provision. It is good for us to hear again what we have already heard.

THE WARNING EXTENDED
In the second verse, Paul warns the Philippians about some "wicked men." "Watch out" is in the imperative and comes from a word meaning "to see" or "to look." It means, "be careful" or "beware."

The apostle uses three phrases to warn the Philippians about those who were perverting the truth of the Word of God. He calls them "dangerous dogs" (3:2, TLB). In our society the dog is a trusted pet, "man's best friend." But in the day in which this was written, dogs roamed in bands and were vicious scavengers. They were a menace to society and a danger to those nearby. When the Jew really wanted to insult someone who wasn't a Jew, he would call him a Gentile dog. That was as low a name as he could give. Paul was saying that the Judaizers, who were calling other men "dogs," were dogs themselves, because they had perverted the gospel of Christ.

He calls them "wicked men" (3:2, TLB). They were immoral in character. They created disorder and unbelief. They were endangering the life of the church by working against the very principles of the life-giving gospel of Christ. They were "evil workers" (KJV).

He also labels them "the false circumcision" (3:2, NASB). This was a play on words in the original language, and a play on words cannot be brought from one language to the other effectively. The word is translated "concision" in the King James Version. We don't recognize that word either, so it doesn't help a great deal. The word literally means "mutilation." In our day we may see pictures of people with scars on their faces or arms because they belong to pagan religions that insist on scarring or mutilating the body as a form of their worship. This is a pagan practice with no spiritual significance.

Paul was saying that the Judaizers thought they were the only ones who had been circumcised, but the truth was that they had merely been mutilated. They had just scarred their bodies. Their circumcision had no value or meaning to their life. It was the same as pagan worship and pagan religion. Any religious rite, when substituted for faith in Christ, is nothing more than meaningless ceremony. They had gone through the motion of religious ritual, but because they did not obey and trust the Lord, it was nothing more than mutilation.

This passage is not a slam at ritual at all. But the point is to not allow ritual in any form to become mere ritual, meaningless and without purpose for our lives. We come mechanically to church without any real hunger for God. We go through the motions of listening and singing and go home untouched by the message of an eternal God. We have allowed the ritual to lose its meaning. Beware of those who would emphasize the legal observance of certain rituals to the exclusion of a commitment of heart to Jesus Christ.

THE DESCRIPTION GIVEN

In verses 3-6 Paul describes true worship or "true circumcision." There are three characteristics of all who are truly obedient to God, those who are the true Israelites. First, all worship is to be guided, controlled, and directed by the Spirit of God (3:3). "It is we who are the circumcision, we who worship in the Spirit of God" (NIV). The *Phillips* paraphrase and *The Jerusalem Bible* give a similar rendering. Any ritual, any form of worship that honors God, is directed by the Spirit of God.

The word "worship" (KJV) is a Greek word which was applied to the ritual rendered by the Jews to God as his chosen people; i.e., the outward worship of God. Whatever ritual a church chooses, whether it be casual and relaxed or very formal and dignified, it needs to be worship "in the Spirit." That is the first characteristic of those who are the true Israel.

Secondly, true worship results in praise for the Lord Jesus. Any worship that is acceptable to God will give glory to Christ. This is in contrast to those who insist on legal observance for its own sake.

The third characteristic of the true circumcision is the realization that we are helpless to save ourselves. We "have no confidence in the flesh" (3:3, KJV). "Flesh" means "that which the flesh produces." The person who really knows the Lord does not put his faith in what he can do. This does not mean that we become passive and do nothing except trust God. It does not mean that we stop using the abilities God gives us. But it means that we do not trust in this alone.

A good illustration is the preparation that we make before a Sunday morning service. We do everything we know to make it a meaningful service. We turn on lights, plug in the organ, print bulletins, etc. But though we do everything we can, we know that unless God touches that service in a special way it will not come alive. We don't sit idly by and wait for God to put an order of service together on the spur of the moment. When someone is saved or when someone is blessed, it is not because of what we did, but because of what God did in working through us. Everything may be in order and everything necessary may be there, but it is all dead without his special touch.

Where does our energy stop and his energy start? Where does our trying and our ability cease and his Spirit take over? God works in us, directing us in our physical and mental effort. When it is all done, we simply must wait for him to put life into what would otherwise be a corpse.

In verses 4-6, Paul says that if anyone could have confidence in the flesh, he surely could. He was circumcised the eighth day, which was as orthodox as one could get. He was of the tribe of Benjamin. (Benjamin was the only son of Jacob born in the Promised Land, and was Jacob's favorite son.)

There were few as Hebrew as Paul. As to the Law, he was a Pharisee. (The Pharisees were the defenders, the interpreters, and the custodians of the Law.) As to zeal, he was a persecutor of the church. No one was more zealous to fight heresy than he. As to legal righteousness, he obeyed all requirements in detail. "Blameless" (3:6, KJV) means more than ceremonial blamelessness or cleanliness. It means that when we put Paul's life next to the moral law of Judaism, he was right at the top. He really measured up. If anyone could have confidence in his own efforts, Paul could. He had unquestionable doctrinal and religious orthodoxy as far as Judaism was concerned. He was a Jew of the Jews.

THE CONCLUSION HE MAKES
"But all these things that I once thought very worthwhile —now I've thrown them all away so that I can put my trust

and hope in Christ alone" (3:7, TLB). There was a time when Paul looked at his righteous life and really thought that it was something. But he met Jesus and simply wrote it all off as loss. All his attainments did not compare with what he had found in Christ. The word translated "thought" means "to consider." It means to pick out that which is superior and place it at the top of the list. He looked at the superiority of his heritage, everything he had achieved in his education and his orthodoxy. But when he looked at Jesus Christ, he counted it all loss and put Jesus at the top instead. What a tremendous conclusion! He looked at all of the ritual, all of his faithfulness to orthodoxy, all of his dedication to purity of doctrine, and his courageous defense of his Jewish faith, but when he added it all up and compared it to Jesus, it was not worth anything. He counted it all loss for the sake of Christ. Only Christ mattered.

Here was a man who had everything, humanly speaking, that a person ought to have, but he didn't have Jesus. When he met Jesus, everything he had faded into insignificance. Only Christ can provide for the needs and the challenges of our lives. Only Jesus can give that which is meaningful and lasting.

17 Seeking
to Know
Christ
Philippians 3:8-11

"YES, EVERYTHING ELSE is worthless when compared with
the priceless gain of knowing Christ Jesus my Lord. I have
put aside all else, counting it worth less than nothing, in
order that I can have Christ, and become one with him, no
longer counting on being saved by being good enough or
by obeying God's laws, but by trusting Christ to save me;
for God's way of making us right with himself depends on
faith—counting on Christ alone. Now I have given up
everything else—I have found it to be the only way to
really know Christ and to experience the mighty power
that brought him back to life again, and to find out what it
means to suffer and to die with him. So, whatever it takes,
I will be one who lives in the fresh newness of life of those
who are alive from the dead" (3:8-11, TLB).

In verse 8, the "everything else" that Paul talked about
was everything he counted significant and precious before
he was saved. He has mentioned some of them in the preceding verses: his heritage, his religious pedigree, his
persecuting the church and being blameless according to
the Law. All of these things he counted loss. Many feel,
and with good reason, that he also referred to the loss of
his property and his family. When Saul of Tarsus became a
Christian, he forfeited the fellowship and support of his

family. His property was likely confiscated, as there is no indication that he continued to have the material position he enjoyed prior to his conversion.

What was it that caused him to count all this loss? It was the surpassing value of knowing Christ Jesus. All the glittering jewels of his prestige and possessions could not compare with knowing "Christ Jesus my Lord" (3:8, TLB). "Lord" speaks of control and ownership, dominance and authority. Jesus Christ controlled Paul's life. Only the Christian can say that the One who dominates him is more precious than anything or anyone else.

The apostle described his achievements outside Christ as "worth less than nothing" (3:8, TLB). This is translated "dung" in the King James Version and "rubbish" in the *New American Standard Bible*. The Greeks used that word to mean "that which is cast to the dogs." In a medical sense, it referred to refuse. It was good for nothing but the garbage heap. That was the value of Paul's legalism and his achievements outside Christ. This speaks of the utter uselessness of keeping the letter of the Law, the futility of trying to please God in our own strength.

Paul uses the present tense, thus speaking of a continual evaluation and examination. "I keep on counting everything that was precious to me to be loss in comparison with the surpassing value of knowing Jesus Christ." "I have put aside all else" is in the aorist tense in the Greek language, which denotes completed action at a point in the past with present implications, but does not speak of continuous action. At a point in the past Paul made a decision to follow Jesus Christ and consequently suffered the loss of all things. After he lost everything, he continued to have the same judgment. In fact, the longer he continued in his relationship to Christ, the more he confirmed his decision to count those things rubbish in order to gain Christ.

EXALTATION

"And become one with him" (3:9, TLB) is in the aorist tense. "That I might become . . ." would be a better translation. It speaks of action at a point in the past and is based on "having Christ." "No longer counting on being saved by being good enough" is in the present tense. Paul is saying that in his B.C. days, his righteousness was based on the Law. When he was saved, the righteousness which comes from God through Christ was given to him on the basis of faith. This is the exaltation of being joined with Christ. This is conversion.

EXPERIENCE

The aorist tense again appears in verse 10: "Now I have given up everything else—I have found it to be the only way to really know Christ and to experience the mighty power that brought him back to life again, and to find out what it means to suffer and to die with him" (TLB). We generally think this is talking about knowing him better. After being a Christian twenty-five or thirty years, the Apostle Paul's driving desire was still to know Christ. But the construction he used here speaks of the conversion experience.

"Know" is the Greek word *"ginōskō"* (to know by personal experience). When Old Testament writers spoke about the sexual relationship of marriage, they would say that a man "knew" his wife. This described the intimate personal relationship of marriage. The Greek equivalent of "knowing one's wife" was *"ginōskō."* For example, we read that Joseph "knew [*ginōskō*] not Mary until she brought forth her firstborn son" (Matt. 1:25).

That is the word used here for knowing Christ. It is in the aorist tense, which speaks of an intimate personal relationship with Christ at a point in the past, but having present implications. *"Ginōskō"* refers to intimate, personal knowledge, not intellectual knowledge. Many know about him, but don't know him.

Verse 10 is a continuation of the thought of verse 9. To know him and the power of his resurrection and the fellowship of his sufferings is all one thought and is all connected to the aorist verb "to know."

The resurrection has power in at least three areas: the power to justify believers (Rom. 4:24, 25), to give assurance of our own bodily resurrection (1 Cor. 15:22ff.), and the power to guarantee that the Lord is always with us (Heb. 13:5, 6). Christ is not dead in a tomb, but he is alive —he lives in us. There is power in the resurrection.

"The fellowship of his sufferings" (KJV) does not refer to Christ's sufferings on the cross but to his sufferings because of godliness. When we suffer for righteousness' sake, we are entering into the sufferings of Christ.

"Being made conformable unto his death" (KJV) could be translated "becoming conformed." Present tense, it speaks of absolute submission to the will of Christ. It refers to a continuous process and a deepening experience. "Conformed" is the same word Paul used in 2:5-8 when he spoke of Jesus Christ "emptying himself" and becoming man on our behalf. We are to be emptied of ourselves until we are full of him. That was what John the Baptist meant when he said, "He must become greater and greater, and I must become less and less" (John 3:30, TLB). We are being conformed to Christ's image and molded in his likeness. That is what makes the Christian faith so exciting.

EXPECTATION
"So, whatever it takes, I will be one who lives in the fresh newness of life of those who are alive from the dead" (3:11,

TLB). "I will be one who lives" is translated "might obtain" in the King James Version and is in the aorist tense. It literally means "to arrive at" or "to come to a place of experiencing something." The word "from the dead" is literally "out from the dead." This refers to the first resurrection.

Because Paul came to know Christ, someday he will arrive at the great privilege of being a part of the resurrection out from the dead. That is a wonderful promise of God to believers. When we place everything the world has to offer alongside knowing Christ, we count it but loss. In the end we will be part of the first resurrection.

18

Reaching for the Prize
Philippians 3:12-14

"I DON'T MEAN TO SAY I am perfect. I haven't learned all I should even yet, but I keep working toward that day when I will finally be all that Christ saved me for and wants me to be. No, dear brothers, I am still not all I should be but I am bringing all my energies to bear on this one thing: Forgetting the past and looking forward to what lies ahead, I strain to reach the end of the race and receive the prize for which God is calling us up to heaven because of what Christ Jesus did for us" (3:12-14, TLB).

In these verses Paul admits that he had not yet become mature in his faith, he is not yet perfect. He then proceeds to draw a picture of an athletic contest and to point out three ingredients necessary for victory. First, there has to be a concentration and purpose. We must decide what we want, put our energies to it, and stick with it. Second, we must rid ourselves of anything that would slow us down. We are to "strip off anything that slows us down or holds us back" (Heb. 12:1). Third, we must put forth continual effort if we are going to win. Paul draws upon these three things as he tells us how to win in the Christian life.

HIS EVALUATION
Few of us ever evaluate our spiritual lives, though we do like to take inventory of each other. We often pass judg-

ment on fellow-Christians. We judge others' dedication or lack of it. We ought to be more concerned about taking personal inventory. In verse 12 and the first part of verse 13 the Apostle Paul makes this evaluation of his Christian life: he has not arrived, he has not achieved everything he ought to have achieved, his love for God was not as deep or as meaningful as it should have been.

This disciple who at one time was very proud of his heritage and his achievements now declares he has not arrived yet. At one time he would have said proudly that he was blameless, he had achieved everything that can be achieved by the standard of the Law. But now he evaluates himself, not in the light of his own human achievement, but in the light of the presence of his Lord. And he plainly declares that he has not become perfect. "Perfect" is a Greek word which does not mean "flawless" or "sinless," but "mature." He is saying, "If my life were a fruit orchard, here and there you would see fruit beginning to form, but it is not yet full-grown. There are signs that something is happening in my life, but I have not yet become mature."

So, he says, "I keep working" (3:12, TLB). That word means "to pursue, to keep after." He is saying that he won't sit back on his laurels or rest on his spiritual experiences of the past. He is pursuing a new goal, but what? This is an interesting phrase in the original, one of the most unusual that can be found anywhere in Scripture. Literally he says, "I am pursuing that I may lay hold of that for which I was laid hold of." He wants to lay hold of what Jesus laid hold of him for. That is bad English, but it is good Greek.

There was a purpose for Paul's salvation (and ours). God had placed his hand upon Paul and chosen him, and Paul wanted to be what he had been called to be, to be available to do what Christ set out to do in him. The King James Version uses the term "apprehended," and that means "arrested." Paul was on the way to Damascus to arrest Christians, but was arrested himself by Jesus Christ. Jesus Christ arrested Paul for a reason, and Paul wanted to experience that reason. He was a man with a one-track mind. He wanted what Jesus wanted for his life, and he pursued it with singleness of purpose and heart.

In verse 13, the phrase "I am still not all I should be" comes from a Greek word which means "to consider." After examining his heart to see what his relationship with God really was like, Paul did not regard himself as having yet laid hold of everything God had for him. He had been the moving force of Christianity in his day. If anyone could pride himself on what he had done, it would be the Apostle Paul. But after looking at the facts, he concluded that he had not fully matured.

How long has it been since we honestly sat down in a private place with an open Bible and an open heart and asked the Lord how we were doing spiritually? Is the Lord pleased with our spiritual progress? We complain about the inefficiency and lack of dedication of others, but we are like the man Jesus told about who observed a speck in his neighbor's eye while he had a beam in his own eye. How much do we really love the Lord? What are our goals in life? We must evaluate ourselves in the light of God's purpose for us.

HIS DETERMINATION

This passage speaks of energy, diligence, discipline. It deals with bringing every energy to bear to serve God. Are we supposed to do that, or is God supposed to do it through us? God works through us, but when he does we will work up a sweat! Many folk would like to twiddle their thumbs and piously say, "I'm going to let God work through me." But remember, when God works through us, he works us.

Paul is talking about our effort and energy being channeled toward a particular goal. "This one thing I do" (3:13, KJV). In the original language the phrase "I do" does not appear. It literally says, "One thing." Only one thing matters; only one thing counts. There is only one goal in life. There is only one reason to love and to serve.

To the church at Corinth Paul said, "I determined not to know any thing among you, save Jesus Christ, and him crucified" (1 Cor. 2:2, KJV). He had a single purpose in life. He pursued one goal. Our difficulty is that we want to do many things. We approach the Christian life like many approach athletics. They can do it all fairly well, but they can't do any of them really well. If we are going to do something excellent, if we are going to excel, we have to concentrate on it. We must determine to wholeheartedly pursue Christ-likeness, being like Jesus. We are to allow his Spirit liberty to build within us character just like that of Jesus Christ. That is our one purpose.

"Forgetting the past and looking forward to what lies ahead . . ." (3:13, TLB). What did Paul forget? He did not forget he was a sinner. He remembered that, so he would remain humble and dependent upon the Lord. He did not forget his mistakes. He remembered them so Satan would not trick him again as he had at other times. What did he forget then? He forgot his success! He forgot the things he once had counted precious. In verses 5, 6 he talked about his heritage and all the achievements he had attained, but he forgot all that.

A young athlete was leading the mile run coming into the home stretch. When he looked over his shoulder to see who was behind him, his one toe caught the heel of the other foot and he stumbled. He did not fall, but he lost enough momentum that the runner in second place passed him and won the race. We can only look back on those we have beaten, on our success, and our looking back will hinder us.

The Apostle Paul says, "I am forgetting those things that lie behind and looking forward to what lies ahead." "Looking forward" pictures the end of a race where two runners are coming to the finish line neck and neck. We can see them strain with every ounce of muscle they have. With every ounce of energy they stretch toward the goal. That is the word Paul uses here.

"I strain to reach the end of the race and receive the prize for which God is calling us up to heaven because of what Christ Jesus did for us" (3:14, TLB). Paul believed his greatest privilege in life was to reach the goal God had set for him. He wanted to be partners with God, to be involved perfectly in the will of God. He pursued that goal with every ounce of energy, with every moment of discipline, with every bit of intelligence.

The greatest temptation that will come our way in our Christian experience will be to worry about 1,001 different things, but we only have one thing to be concerned about: are we like Jesus? Have we kept our eyes on him? Whatever takes our eyes off him is drawing us away from God's purpose in our lives, for it is his purpose to make us like him.

Living
by God's
Standards
Philippians 3:15-17

THIS PASSAGE is a great corrective to those who are satisfied with their spiritual progress to date. However many things God has done with our lives in the past, there is still more to be done. However many achievements we may have reached in the past, there is still more to reach for in the future. Verses 12-17 remind us of the hunger that ought to be in our souls for spiritual things. We must press on and pursue the things of the Lord.

"I hope all of you who are mature Christians will see eye-to-eye with me on these things, and if you disagree on some point, I believe that God will make it plain to you—if you fully obey the truth you have. Dear brothers, pattern your lives after mine and notice who else lives up to my example" (3:15-17, TLB).

PERFECTION

God has a standard that he wants us to adopt as a pattern for life, and we see it in these verses: perfection. In verse 15 he says, "Let us therefore, as many as be perfect..." (KJV). But in verse 12 he had said, "not as though I had already attained, either were already perfect" (KJV). It seems rather strange that the man who had denied perfection in verse 12 now claims it in verse 15. The key to understanding this seeming contradiction is to understand what the word "perfect" means. It is a very elastic term that can cover many things. It can mean "mature, having realized the end or the purpose for which a thing was intended or created."

In verse 12 Paul was simply stating that he had not become completely mature. That is the elastic stretching of the word to get his point across. But in verse 15 he was using perfection to mean the opposite of childishness, or what one writer calls "the spirit of the infantile."

There is no question that the Apostle Paul considered himself to be spiritually adult. "It's like this: when I was a child I spoke and thought and reasoned as a child does. But when I became a man my thoughts grew far beyond those of my childhood, and now I have put away the childish things" (1 Cor. 13:11, TLB). Perfection or maturity contrasts with a childish spirit. A mature mind recognizes that there is still much to learn. One who is truly mature is the first to recognize that he has just scratched the surface of knowledge and understanding. In his maturity, Paul faced squarely his immaturity.

The Philippians were admonished to see "eye-to-eye" with Paul. He is talking about the perspective that he has just described in verses 13, 14. He is referring to the attitude of not regarding himself as having reached full maturity, but forgetting what lies behind and reaching forward to what lies ahead, and thus pressing on to the prize of the high calling of Christ Jesus. Those of us who are mature must live realizing that we must always be reaching forward. We cannot rest on our past achievements. We must pursue the prize that God had put before us. We must reach toward maturity.

"And if you disagree on some point, I believe God will make it plain to you" (3:15, TLB). This is one of the most unusual statements I find anywhere in the New Testament. Paul is saying, "If anyone thinks any differently than I do, they are wrong, but God will show them and I am going to be patient with them." There is a need for that kind of attitude in the Christian fellowship today. So many of us who are growing and maturing spiritually get impatient with those who aren't growing. We want to write them off. There are many who play with rituals, but do not worship. There are many who count their merits, but forget to praise the Savior. But such as these were considered patiently because God would reveal the truth to them in time. God would show them the right way.

He is not saying that God will give some new Scripture, some new truth, but a new inward revelation of the inspired Word. New light will dawn. Not new Scripture, but a new understanding of the Scripture will come. It is the gentle work of the Holy Spirit to bring a deeper understanding of the Word of God.

One of my favorite pastimes is to go back through my old sermons. I wonder about some of them! I thank God for the churches I have served that put up with me and loved me. I have learned so much more than I knew when I preached those sermons. New light has come. Sometimes there has been a complete reversal of how I understood a passage of Scripture. The beautiful thing is that if we are preaching the Word, God's Holy Spirit will apply the Word to every one of us at that particular point of maturity where we are.

I do not have to think up clever ideas when I am sharing the Word of God. My sermons are very vanilla, very bland. There is nothing exciting about them. But if I am preaching the Word of God, God will reveal what it means. And what it means for us today may be a different angle from what it meant to us a year ago. When a man is facing life spiritually as an adult, God will lead him in the truth.

Notice the words Paul uses in these passages: "I keep

working" (3:12), "I am bringing all my energies to bear" (3:13), "I strain to reach" (3:14). We are involved in a holy and strenuous struggle. If we stumble and err in our judgment, God will tenderly lead us back to the right way. If our heart is right, God will protect us. If we love him with all of our hearts and want his Word to be rightly divided in our hearts, God will bring to us the insight that is needed. When we fall by the wayside or have faulty judgment, God will bring our erring feet back onto the solid path.

PERFORMANCE

Paul continues, "if you fully obey the truth you have" (3:16, TLB). The basic analogy in this passage is that of an athletic contest. Here he simply says that we need to obey the rules. If an athlete in the process of training for Olympic activity does not train properly, he is often disqualified from the race. If in the race he exerts every energy and wins the race, but violates the rules, he is disqualified. He does not lose his citizenship, though he greatly embarrasses his country. He does, however, lose his right to win the prize.

Those of us who are facing life as spiritually mature adults need to live by the rules. We need to live up to the light we have, do what we know to do. "Follow the Lord's rules for doing his work, just as an athlete either follows the rules or is disqualified and wins no prize" (2 Tim. 2:5, TLB).

In the Olympic Games, the judge would disqualify one who didn't run by the rules. It mattered little what the runner thought or what the spectators thought; it was what the judge said that counted. It is interesting that when Paul said we all are going to have to appear before the judgment seat of Christ (Rom. 14:10), the word translated "judgment seat" is the Greek word *"bēma,"* the very same word used to refer to the place where the Olympic judges gave out the prizes. We must play by the rules. We must live by God's standard.

If we leave the way we know or fail to live up to the light we have, we are in dangerous territory. Any child of God who is deliberately compromising and deliberately rebelling against God needs to realize that he is in great peril.

PERCEPTION

"Dear brothers, pattern your lives after mine and notice who else lives up to my example" (3:17, TLB). Paul is telling the Philippians to watch him and to watch those who ought to be living for Jesus. "Pattern your lives after mine" literally means "keep on imitating me." The verb is in a continuous present tense. "You are to keep on following my example." It seems as though the Apostle Paul is bragging on himself, but if we have followed him all the way through, we know that such is not the spirit with which he says it. We know that he doesn't claim to be a superhero or a supersaint. He confessed that he was the chief of sinners. Paul never spoke from a superior pose. He was simply saying, "God has shown me the direction life ought to take. Now you follow God's leading too."

No teaching is very effective unless what is taught is true in the life of the teacher. The old maxim "Do what I say and not what I do" never has worked and never will. Paul is saying, "I am not telling you to do something that I don't do. I am walking down the same path. I am doing what I am telling you to do. Follow my example."

He goes on to tell them to "notice who else lives up to my example." In this matter of the Christian being an example, we do not really have a choice. Whether we like it or not, we are examples. When we gave our hearts to Jesus Christ, we became examples to others of what Jesus is like. Our choice is not whether we will be an example, but whether we are going to be a good or bad one.

When I was a student, God revealed to me that I was to be an example in my classroom work. So I increased my "C's" to "A's." I didn't make straight "A's" because I was brilliant, but because suddenly it dawned on me that I was an example to other students of what a Christian student ought to be like. I wanted to please the One whose example I was following. That transferred into every area of my life, including my home life. When others were rebelling and being disrespectful, I endeavored to honor the responsibility given to me. I had a responsibility to be an example.

We are all in the same boat. We may not like being an example, but we do not have a choice. Are we going to point men to Jesus and be a good example, or are we going to point men to Satan and be an example of everything a Christian should not be? That is our choice.

20

Enemies
of the Cross
Philippians 3:18-21

THE BOOK OF Philippians has been called "the epistle of joy." "Rejoice," "joy," and "joyous" appear over and over again in this book. But when we come to these verses, we see weeping, sadness, and sorrow.

"For I have told you often before, and I say it again now with tears in my eyes, there are many who walk along the Christian road who are really enemies of the cross of Christ. Their future is eternal loss, for their god is their appetite: they are proud of what they should be ashamed of; and all they think about is this life here on earth. But our homeland is in heaven, where our Savior the Lord Jesus Christ is; and we are looking forward to his return from there. When he comes back he will take these dying bodies of ours and change them into glorious bodies like his own, using the same mighty power that he will use to conquer all else everywhere" (3:18-21, TLB).

OUR ENEMIES
In verse 18 the Apostle Paul refers to "enemies of the cross." Many believe he was talking about the gnostics, antinomians who believed in the deification of human flesh and in living for lustful, sensual pleasure. However,

it seems more likely that he is talking not about pagans outside the church, but about those who claim to know Christ. They profess to be Christians, but they are not saved. He was probably talking about the Judaizers, who insisted that it was necessary to keep the Mosaic Law in addition to having faith in Christ in order to be saved. In this sense, they were enemies of the cross.

When Christ died, the veil of the temple was torn in half, from top to bottom. It was as though God was saying, "You no longer need traditions and the legalism of Judaism. A perfect sacrifice has been offered." The cross of Jesus Christ became the eternal sacrifice for our sins. But these Judaizers claimed that the cross was not sufficient. They came to add to the burden of those who wanted to be saved by adding the Law of Moses to the work of redemption that Christ wrought on the cross. In addition to this, they lived immoral lives. They used their so-called Christianity to justify their sinful life-style.

There were two sets of people to whom this applied. First, there were those who distorted their Christian liberty. They said that in Christianity all law was gone and they could live as they pleased. It did not matter what they did. Another group distorted the doctrine of grace. They said that since grace covers all of our sins, sin as much as you like— grace will cover it. These Judaizers claimed to be Christians, yet used their Christianity as a cloak for immorality, gluttonous behavior, and rebellion against God. In effect, they sought to put a yoke of bondage around the lives of those who would follow Christ.

Verse 18 (TLB) mentions "many who walk along the Christian road." The word "walk" involves behavior. It speaks of how they lived, their deportment, the manner in which they carried on their lives. If we follow closely, we will find that the way they lived describes many of the people in the church today.

"For I have told you often before, and I say it again now

with tears in my eyes . . ." (3:18, TLB). In this epistle of joy Paul is weeping. Was he crying because his circumstances had overwhelmed him? No. Because his heart was fixed on Christ, no circumstance could destroy his joy. Was he weeping because he had been mistreated by these Roman Christians? No. He would not let other people rob him of his joy. Why, then, was he weeping? Because he saw people who claimed to know Jesus Christ, yet were living lives that denied the reality of Jesus Christ. He was not weeping for himself. It broke his heart when he saw professing Christians living the way they lived.

Before we proceed any further, we need to examine our own attitudes when we view the lives of professing Christians. We often indict them with delight. We enjoy picking apart the lives of other people who claim to be Christians. We gossip about their frailties, their disloyalties, their defiled garments. We gloat over their failures. We do not weep.

It would be better for us to leave our brother's sins alone and not even name them unless our warning to them is bathed in our tears. Paul had some hard things to say, but he was weeping. His bluntness was bathed in tears.

"Their future is eternal loss" (3:19, TLB). "Eternal loss" is the translation of one Greek word which could be translated "waste" or "lostness." This speaks of a wasted life, an eternity of destruction, losing everything that makes life meaningful. The end of a person's life who professes Christ but who does not possess him is destruction. It is just the opposite of salvation.

"Their god is their appetite." They lived for sensual pleasure. Whatever felt good, they did it. This speaks of immorality, gluttony, and all things associated with physical excesses. It describes someone whose life is conquered and controlled by physical appetites. Their god is their stomach, their appetite, their physical desires. What a tragic description!

But it gets even worse. "They are proud of what they should be ashamed of." They bragged about how indulgent and sensual they were.

"And all they think about is this life here on earth." They lived only for this world. There was no time in their lives for the world to come, for eternity. By choosing to live only for the present, they destroyed every hope of ever living happily in the future. No wonder Paul wept.

OUR CITIZENSHIP

As weak and frail as we as Christians often are, as many times as we stumble and fail in our Christian lives, even then the Christian life is a refreshing contrast. It is not a life lived for sensual pleasure and with only the fulfillment of fleshly, carnal appetites. Even the weakest Christian is on a higher plane than that.

"Our homeland is in heaven" (3:20, TLB). "Homeland" is a Greek word from which we get our word "politics" and speaks of our behavior as citizens of a country. This would have special meaning to the people in Philippi, because Philippi was a Roman colony. Philippi, though separated from Rome, was Rome in miniature. Roman law governed it. When a baby was born in Philippi, his name was recorded in Rome and he was a citizen of Rome.

When Paul talked to the Philippians about their citizenship being in heaven, they could understand how though they were separated from heaven, they were a colony of heaven. They did not belong to the society around them. They did not belong to the paganism and godlessness around them. Their real homeland was heaven.

There is a sacred pride in the fact that we are children of God, joint heirs with Jesus Christ. We bear the birthmark of heaven. A man who belongs to Christ marches to a different drummer and obeys different orders. His citizenship is not on this earth, but in heaven.

OUR SAVIOR

Paul declares that Christ is coming from heaven. Sometimes we look to earth for our provision, but our Savior is coming from heaven. "We are looking forward" refers to eager, earnest expectation, fervent desire. There is tremendous energy in the present power of a future hope. Think of how many people's lives are driven by something they hope for in the future. Every time that young PGA golfer tees up on the first tee of the tournament, he has a hope he is going to win that tournament. That is what keeps him going. Every time a young rookie comes to a football or baseball game, he has a hope of being a star, making the team, contributing to it. It is that hope that drives him. Every young businessman who starts in a business venture has hope, and the power of that future hope has present power in his life.

Abraham looked for a city (Heb. 11:10), and because he looked for a city he was content to live in a tent all his life. Moses, because he looked for rewards in glory, because he viewed earthly pleasures as not being comparable to the anticipation of what was to come, forsook the material possessions of this world. Even our Lord, because of the joy of his anticipation of the victory, endured the shame of the cross. The Apostle Paul had great possessions, but he had greater expectations. He eagerly awaited his Savior, the Lord Jesus Christ. That is the blessed hope of the Christian.

Scripture tells us to be looking for Christ's return. There is to be an air of expectancy. Whether he is coming soon or not, we must be ready.

What will happen when he comes? "When he comes
back he will take these dying bodies of ours and change
them into glorious bodies like his own, using the same
mighty power that he will use to conquer all else everywhere" (3:21, TLB). The word "change" refers to complete
change. He is not talking about just reviving our bodies.
He is going to transform them. He is not just going to
raise our old bodies and resuscitate them, but change
them completely. The words "change them into glorious
bodies like his own" speak of outward appearance. Our
present body is just our traveling dress. Someday there
is going to be a marriage feast of the Lamb, and we will
have to get dressed for the occasion. Rather than being
temporal and purely physical, our new bodies will be
eternalized, immortalized. They will be conformed to
him. We will put on our bridal attire for our meeting with
our Lord at his appearing.

He does this by "using the same mighty power that he
will use to conquer all else everywhere." The word "conquer" means to "arrange in rank, to arrange in proper
order." In this world we get everything out of order, but
when Jesus Christ comes again, he will put everything in
its place. Today our values are twisted and we do not live
by right priorities. But when Jesus comes back, he is going
to arrange everything in its proper order, and he is going
to do it by the exertion of his power. "Mighty power" is
one word in the original language, the Greek word
"dunamis." We get our word "dynamite" from it.

More exciting than that anticipation is the fact that we
can appropriate his great power today. We know that
someday every knee will bow to Jesus and every tongue
will confess that he is Lord. But we can bow our knees
now. We can let him put everything in proper perspective
today. He doesn't want us to just exist, to drift along at the

mercy of circumstances. He wants to put everything in its proper place and give life meaning and balance. He will do it when he returns, and he does it when he comes into our hearts.

WHEN WE COME to this passage, we come to one of the problems that existed in the church at Philippi: disharmony. Two women apparently had had a disagreement. We do not know what the disagreement was about or what was the source of the dissension, but remember: issues do not make quarrels; people make quarrels. People may use issues as a reason or an excuse for a quarrel, but the people themselves are ultimately the causes.

"Dear brother Christians, I love you and long to see you, for you are my joy and my reward for my work. My beloved friends, stay true to the Lord. And now I want to plead with those two dear women, Euodias and Syntyche. Please, please, with the Lord's help, quarrel no more—be friends again. And I ask you, my true teammate, to help these woman, for they worked side by side with me in telling the Good News to others; and they worked with Clement, too, and the rest of my fellow workers whose names are written in the Book of Life. Always be full of joy in the Lord; I say it again, rejoice!" (4:1-4, TLB).

The church at Philippi began with a women's prayer meeting. There is a good chance that Euodias and Syntyche were part of that original group. There is every reason to believe that they were devout sincere women who had the best interest of the gospel at heart—". . .for they worked side by side with me in telling the Good News to others." This tells us that common faith in Christ and a common desire to serve the Lord does not necessarily resolve personal differences. Often human pride, stubbornness, etc. are too obvious in our lives. It is good for us to realize that very sincere people who love the Lord and love the Lord's work can disagree, sometimes disagreeably.

There are three phrases in these verses that are keys to understanding the passage: "Stay true to the Lord" (4:1), "with the Lord's help...be friends again" (4:2), and "be full of joy in the Lord" (4:4). Everything is determined by the phrase "in the Lord" or its equivalent. The only way we can properly stand for what is right is to stand in the Lord. The only way we can properly agree and live in harmony is in the Lord. The only way we can truly rejoice is in the Lord.

STAY TRUE

Looking at the phrase "stay true to the Lord," notice that Paul begins by saying, "Dear brother Christians," a phrase of deep love and affection. This is not just a general greeting, but an expression of affectionate energy. He genuinely loves them and is seeking to guide them in a needed area. "Dear brother Christians, I love you and long to see you." Love is always accompanied by desire. He loved them and he desired to help them, to counsel them.

He calls them "my joy and my reward." His joy was in seeing his converts stand firm in the faith, seeing his converts move forward for the Lord. He delighted in seeing others succeed, in seeing them do well. He had seen them move from darkness to light. He had heard their songs of blessing, excitement, and jubilee. He had watched them grow and mature.

"His reward" is the Greek word for "crown." Two words in the Greek language were commonly used for crown. One referred to a royal crown, a kingly crown, but the word used here is the Greek word "*stephanos*," which refers to a victor's crown. The victor's crown was made of olive leaves with parsley and bay leaves entertwined in it. It was the goal all athletes wanted to win. That crown was the climax of their efforts. This crown was also used at particularly festive banquets to honor the guests. It is as though the Apostle Paul was saying, "You Philippians are my crown. I find my greatest joy and reward in you. You are the victor's crown for me."

On the basis of this, he now told them to "stay true to the Lord." If they were to be triumphant, they must stand in the Lord. Every time we stand in our own strength, we suffer defeat. Any time we stand in our own ability, we will fail.

BE FRIENDS AGAIN

"With the Lord's help, quarrel no more—be friends again" (4:2, TLB). Paul is telling Euodias and Syntyche that their quarrel cannot be ignored. It must be dealt with. And it will. Problems in families, friendships, and fellowships usually stem from little things that are left alone and soon become a breach that cannot be bridged. Personal differences often breed social division. Paul is telling us nothing is to separate us from each other. We are to live in harmony in the Lord.

"And I ask you, my true teammate, to help these women" (4:3, TLB). Who is he talking to? There have been many conjectures, but no one really knows. Some have suggested that the word "teammate" is a proper name and that Paul is naming someone who is particularly prominent in the church. We cannot know for certain. But at any rate we see that he is asking a trusted friend, a true teammate, to be a peacemaker. A sympathetic friend can many times reconcile differences between Christian people.

These women had faithfully proclaimed the gospel. They were involved in the ministry of the church. Paul is saying, "They were faithful to us in spreading the gospel. Now we must be faithful in helping them resolve their differences."

Then he mentions Clement, a very prominent man in the church, and "the rest of my fellow workers whose names are written in the Book of Life" (4:3, TLB). Paul mentions the prominent and the obscure, the leaders and the rank and file of the church. He mobilizes the entire church to mend the breech in the fellowship. It is as though he were saying, "There is no effort too great to maintain peace in the church."

We are far too quick to divide ourselves into factions. Most of the time the division comes because of our selfish desire to vindicate ourselves. Something happens which we take as a personal affront, so we set out to justify ourselves. Unfortunately, we cannot justify our actions without casting discredit upon the actions of someone else. Selfishness comes to the forefront, Christ is dethroned, and a schism develops. A quarreling church does not please God.

Paul is telling every member of the church to work together to help. Perhaps the best peacemakers in the church may be the most obscure members. This is not a work just for the leadership. When we get to heaven, the folks who will get the greatest rewards may not be those we hear the most about, but those who lived in obscurity, in the shadows. God may have kept them in the background so he could produce more fragrant fruit in their lives. Perhaps God's strongest followers do not care who gets the credit. They are obscure, but vital to the work of the church. Perhaps harmony in the Philippian church came, not through the trusted friend that he called upon or Clement or any of the very prominent members, but rather through those who were just referred to as "the rest of my fellow workers whose names are written in the Book of Life."

Our greatest joy ought to be that our names are written in the Book of Life. The Gospel of Luke shares the story of the seventy who came back rejoicing because the devils were subject to them. Jesus told them not to rejoice because of that, but because their names are written in heaven (Luke 10:20). We rejoice about the good things that happen to us. We rejoice about the opportunities that we are given, about the successes we achieve. But our greatest rejoicing ought to be that our names are recorded in heaven. Our greatest delight should be that we belong to Christ.

BE FULL OF JOY

The book of Philippians is written by an old man who is in prison. If anyone didn't have anything humanly speaking to be happy about, he would be the one. He knows he may die very soon, and he is in jail. Yet his epistle is an epistle of joy. That tells us that Christian joy is not dependent upon our immediate circumstances.

There are many who will serve the Lord as long as everything goes well, as long as they have money in the bank, health, and everything they want. But when circumstances change, their faith fades. Paul tells us that we are to rejoice in the Lord *always.* Hard circumstances had not made him hard. The Apostle Paul tells us to give thanks to the Lord *in* all things (1 Thess. 5:18), and to give thanks *for* all things (Eph. 5:20). There is no circumstance in which we cannot rejoice in the Lord.

Our rejoicing is "in the Lord." We are to get our joy from

him—not from serving him, not from pleasing him, not from worshiping him, but from him. The Christian who is dependent upon the work of the Lord for his joy will soon find his joy crumbling beneath him. Our joy is in the Lord.

Our joy is not in the things we do for Christ, but in him, just him. Is it easier to talk *about* the Lord or *to* the Lord? Do we find it easier to talk about the Bible or to read the Bible? Do we find it easier to lay our burdens upon the saints in the prayer room or upon the Lord? If our joy is not in Christ, something is going to happen to take the joy away. If our joy is in husband or wife, something may happen to husband or wife and then where will our joy be? If our joy is in our children, something may happen to our children and where will our joy be? "Rejoice in the Lord alway" (4:4, KJV).

22

Freedom from Anxiety
Philippians 4:5-7

IT IS INTERESTING that these verses come immediately on the heels of, "Always be full of joy in the Lord; I say it again, rejoice!" Now Paul speaks about kindness, gentleness, confidence, freedom from worry and anxiety. Rejoicing is closely related to not worrying. When we rejoice, our worries leave. Worry and anxiety are enemies of joy. And if we do not have joy in our lives, we will not be the kind of gracious, gentle people we ought to be.

"Unselfish" in verse 5 means graciousness, reasonableness, kindness, submitting our rights to others because of sympathy and love. A person who is joy-filled is kind. But a person who is harsh and abrasive, who is basically disruptive in his own life and in the fellowship of others, is a person who does not know joy.

"Let everyone see that you are unselfish and considerate in all you do. Remember that the Lord is coming soon. Don't worry about anything; instead, pray about everything; tell God your needs and don't forget to thank him for his answers. If you do this you will experience God's peace, which is far more wonderful than the human mind can understand. His peace will keep your thoughts and your hearts quiet and at rest as you trust in Christ Jesus" (4:5-7, TLB).

CONSIDERATION

In verse 5 the key word is "considerate," or literally "able to yield." Some translate it "forbearance, graciousness." It simply means to think of other people, going out of our way to see that someone else has their rights rather than demanding ours. We don't do it because we have to, but because in our heart there is a love that controls our lives and causes us to be concerned for them. Paul is encouraging personal consideration of other people. This is the opposite of stubbornness, arrogance, thoughtlessness.

The perfect example of this attitude is found in the second chapter of Philippians where we read that Jesus was in the form of God, yet made himself of no reputation. He voluntarily emptied himself of his rights in his consideration for others. He gave himself. He who was equal with God became man, limiting himself, for us. "Let this same mind be in you, which was also in Christ Jesus" (2:5, KJV). That is the emphasis of this verse. "Let your gracious gentleness, your sweet reasonableness, your yielding spirit be known to all men."

Paul says that *all* men ought to be the object of our sweetness, our kindness, our reasonableness. We ought to yield our rights toward everyone. We like to yield our rights to people we love, but we do not like to yield our rights to people we do not like. Our spirit of loving concern ought to be demonstrated even to those who create hostility in our hearts. Why do so many churches have dissension? Because people demand their rights. Our sweet reasonableness must be experienced by all men.

The reason Paul admonishes us to do this is because "the Lord is coming soon." The reason I can yield my rights to you is because I know that the One who is the true Judge of all the actions and motives of men is soon to come, and I know he is going to deal rightly with me. If we live our lives in anticipation of the return of the Lord, it will help us to have a Christlike character and disposition.

The early church lived in an expectancy of the return of the Lord. Interspersed throughout the epistles are such statements as, "The Lord is at hand," "the Lord will return." If we anticipate that the Lord who judges our hearts, thoughts, and intents will come soon, then we will want our lives to be such that he can give a good report when he comes.

CONFIDENCE
"Don't worry about anything; instead, pray about everything; tell God your needs and don't forget to thank him for his answers" (4:6, TLB). The phrase "don't worry about anything" speaks of a confidence that God will bring his purposes to bear in our lives. We will not be abandoned. The Lord will keep his hand upon us. We do not need to be anxious because we are in his hands. God is still God.

"Worry" literally means "to be pulled in opposite directions." Do you get the picture? Our hopes pull us one way and our fears pull us another. We are torn apart by the cares that are in our lives. This is a present imperative in the original language, and if we put "never" in there we get a more accurate picture. *"Never* worry about anything."

How do we not worry? Paul doesn't just say, "We will pray about it." He uses three words to describe how we are to pray about it. If we want the kind of prayer that banishes worry, the kind that evaporates anxiety, then this passage of Scripture is for us. Paul says, "Pray about everything" (4:6, TLB). "Pray" is a general word for prayer, speaking of praise, devotion, adoration, and worship. It does not speak of the words which we say, but of the spirit with which we pray. Prayer never begins with words. It begins in the heart, with an attitude toward God. If we are to worry about nothing, we must praise and worship God.

Paul goes on, "Tell God your needs." This means an earnest sharing of our needs and problems. Once we have come to God in a spirit of praise and devotion, then we can tell him what the problem is. We can share our needs, itemize them. We need to be specific in our prayers. We should not just ask him to meet our needs, but tell him which ones. This word, translated "supplication" in the King James Version, means an earnest sharing of the problem. We are to share with God what the difficulty is. Is it finances? Tell him. Is it fellowship or stress within the home? Talk to him about those difficulties and stress. Is it vocational pressure? Tell him about it. Is it a lost loved one? Share that with him.

Next Paul says, "And don't forget to thank him for his answers." So we have adoration, supplication, and then appreciation. Every prayer ought to have in it thanksgiving to God. What a privilege it is for finite, sinful human beings to be able to relate to the eternal God of the universe!

A basic element of thanksgiving is submission to God. If we are grateful to God, we are submissive to him. An element of gratitude is being able to pray, "Lord, I am willing for you to do what pleases you. I am willing for you to have your way in my life."

"Never be anxious for anything, but keep on making your requests known to God in everything." It is exciting to know that God is concerned about everything we are concerned about. In fact, God is more concerned about it than we are. There is nothing we can't talk to him about. There is nothing too great for his power to handle, nothing so small that his grace is unconcerned. He never gets tired of our letting him know what is in our hearts. We don't tell him because he doesn't know, but we tell him to allow him to enter into those problems and bring about a solution. We tell him so that we can enter into a new relationship with him.

CONFINEMENT

"If you do this you will experience God's peace, which is far more wonderful than the human mind can understand. His peace will keep your thoughts and your hearts quiet and at rest as you trust in Christ Jesus" (4:7, TLB). The key word here is the word "keep," a Greek word which means "to guard." The noun form of the verb means "a garrison" or "a fortress." In a garrison we are protected. We have a defense, someone to shield us from danger. We are guarded. That is the word Paul uses here. God's peace will keep, will guard, will confine our hearts and minds.

"God's peace" is the peace which God produces, the peace which comes from God. It is different from man's peace. Jesus said, "I am leaving you with a gift—peace of mind and heart! And the peace I give isn't fragile like the peace the world gives. So don't be troubled or afraid" (John 14:27, TLB). Man's peace generally means the absence of friction or the absence of problems, calmness, no difficulties, no one bothering us. But the peace of God means that everything is functioning as it is supposed to function. Everything is perfectly at ease in the midst of turmoil. God's peace is not an orchestra where all of the instruments are quiet, but it is an orchestra where all of the instruments are in tune and playing a symphony together, playing in harmony together. This is not a peace that is detached from the world, like a monastery removed from society, but a peace that causes life to go on in the midst of

the turmoil and confusion of this world. That is the peace
that God gives.

Paul describes God's peace this way: " . . .far more wonderful than the human mind can understand." This
means that no one can really comprehend the peace of
God, but more important it means that the peace of God
that passes all understanding is a peace that the mind of
man cannot produce. We think that to be free of care, we
have to have a nice place to live, money in the bank, all the
bills paid, and everyone healthy. But people who have all
those things still do not have that kind of peace. No
amount of conniving, scheming, or planning by man can
produce this peace. It is more than the human mind can
produce.

This peace "will keep your thoughts and hearts quiet
and at rest as you trust in Christ Jesus." The peace of God
stands guard over the two areas where worry begins—our
hearts and our minds. Wrong thinking is in the mind;
wrong feeling is in the heart. When we think wrong, we
worry. When we feel wrong, we worry. The peace of God
stands guard in our hearts and minds.

Remember that when the Apostle Paul wrote this, he
was chained to a guard twenty-four hours a day. That
guard walked beside him, sat beside him, stood beside
him, slept beside him. Here Paul is saying, "Your heart
and your mind are chained to the peace of God." Whether
we stand or sit, rejoice or mourn, God's peace guards us.

"Heart" is the Greek word which speaks of the whole
inner being. It speaks of the understanding, the affection,
the will. So the peace of God guards our understanding,
our affections, and our wills.

God, through Jesus Christ, has made it possible for us to
experience a worry-free, carefree life with deep peace in
our hearts. It comes when we bow our knee and claim him
as our Savior and Lord.

Doing the Best Things

23

Philippians 4:8, 9

WE ARE CONFRONTED here with the importance of thinking about the right things. Here is a law of life we dare not miss. If we think about something long enough and often enough, we soon will not be able to stop thinking about it. Whatever we dwell upon in our thoughts soon shapes our lives. What we think about, we end up doing, for thought and action are inevitably connected. Worry, anxiety, and care are expressions of dwelling upon the wrong things in our minds. On the other hand, a revolution in our thought life will inevitably result in a revolution in our lives.

"And now, brothers, as I close this letter let me say this one more thing: Fix your thoughts on what is true and good and right. Think about things that are pure and lovely, and dwell on the fine, good things in others. Think about all you can praise God for and be glad about. Keep putting into practice all you learned from me and saw me doing, and the God of peace will be with you" (4:8, 9, TLB).

CONTEMPLATION

In verse 8 the Apostle Paul lists for us the things that ought to occupy our minds and hearts. The word "true" does not just mean truth in its simplest form, such as two plus two equals four. The word used here implies eternal truth, that which is absolutely true. It refers to the great, true principles of life: love, compassion, integrity, etc.

We are to dwell on that which is "good." Other translations render this "honest" or "honorable." It means something that has the dignity of holiness upon it, something that is worthy of respect, that which has a serious purpose. It has with it the connotation of dwelling upon things that build our self-respect. One of the greatest needs spiritually today is to have self-respect and to build self-esteem from God's perspective.

We are to fix our thoughts on those things that are "right." This is the Greek word *dikaios*. From that word we get our word "righteous." It means in its original context a "righteous man, a just man." Such a man faces his duty and does it. He gives proper respect to both God and man. This speaks of right relationship and proper action. We are to think on those things that are right and proper, those things of duty and responsibility. We ought to contemplate those things that cause us to be right with God and with each other.

Then we are urged to continually think upon things that are "pure," a word which means "moral purity." One of the great temptations of the first century was that of moral impurity because of illicit sexual relationships encouraged in the worship of pagan gods. From my studies of history and my observations of the present, I must conclude that there has never been a day when there has been such temptation to moral impurity as there is today. Think about the things that are pure, and do not become involved with moral impurity.

Consider those things that are "lovely," a word that could be translated "winsome" or that which calls forth love. It is that quality that causes love to respond to it. Think about *those* things. We are to think about the things that reach down within our hearts and cause us to respond in love.

"Dwell on the fine, good things in others." "Good things" literally means "fair speaking." The word seems to go back to a pagan practice. At the altar of a pagan god, at the point when the sacrifice was being offered, there was always in the Greek world a time of silence. It was as though the only thing to be heard was that which was worthy of the gods who were to be appeased. The word can be translated, "Think upon those things that are fit for God to hear."

There are too many ugly words and too many impure words in vocabularies in our world today. Can we not imagine what a wonderful improvement our society would have if the only words spoken were words fit for God to hear? The words upon our lips and the thoughts in our minds ought to please God. Even many Christian people fail tragically here. There is no place in the vocabulary or the thoughts of a Christian for ugly, false, or impure words. There is no place for words that are degrading. There is no place for blasphemous slang. There is no possible justification for a man to say things like that. Paul says, "Whatever things are worthy for God to hear, think about those things, because if you think about them you will say them."

"If there be any virtue . . ." (4:8, KJV). "Virtue" means "excellence." In classical Greek, the word referred to any kind of excellence. It could be the excellence of a farmer harvesting his crops, or the excellence of a tool performing its job, or the excellence of a lawyer. As we come into Christian usage, the idea of excellence applies to spiritual excellence and spiritual virtue. Virtuous things are those things that can enhance our relationship with God, that can lift us to the holy of holies, that can improve and mature our fellowship with God. We are to think on such things.

The King James Version continues, "if there be any praise . . . ." Some feel man should not seek praise. But there is nothing wrong with praising others. In fact, we are uplifted and encouraged by the praise of others. This verse speaks of moral praise or approbation. When we think upon these things, perhaps it is our own heart that praises us. Or perhaps a friend will commend us, or God himself will approve us as we think upon these things.

What we think about long enough and often enough will ultimately become an obsession, a passion, and an action in our lives. So our minds must be made to dwell upon good things, excellent things. Any one of us could sit down and think about enough problems to have a nervous breakdown. If we dwell upon the difficulties in our lives long enough, they will absolutely destroy us. It is imperative that we think about right things.

John Hunter once said that our minds are like great television screens that we can never turn off. When we are asleep they are still going. Our subconscious is operating. There is always something on the screens of our minds. If we were watching a questionable television program and we couldn't turn it off, what would be our only other choice? To change channels. That is exactly what the Apostle Paul is telling us to do. "Don't dwell upon those things which will destroy you. Change the channel."

To do that requires discipline. This is one of the reasons why we ought to memorize Scripture. "Thy word have I hid in mine heart, that I might not sin against thee" (Psa. 119:11, KJV). What is not of faith is sin; so whenever we do not have faith, whenever care and anxiety and worry and depression set in, it is sin. But we can change channels. We can put God's Word in our hearts.

The book of Acts tells about a group of people who burned over $10,000 worth of books (Acts 19:19), because they were godless books, books that hurt their spiritual relationship with God. It is distressing to go into hospital rooms and find cheap novels and magazines there. What we put into our minds will control us. When we read suggestive magazines and novels that dwell on sex and immorality, we program our minds in that direction. When we put such trash within us, we destroy our spiritual happiness and progress. Then when we come to a pressure point, we fall to pieces because we have fed our minds the garbage that comes out of the sordid materials of our society. "Whatsoever things are true, honest, just, pure, lovely, or of good report, think on *these* things."

CONDUCT

"Keep putting into practice all you learned from me and saw me doing..." (4:9, TLB). Many Christians are spiritual eggheads! They are brilliant spiritually, but have no practical expression of that knowledge. Knowledge is not meant for our heads; it is meant for our hearts. What is in our heart will determine how we live and what we do.

The verbs in verse 9 are all aorist verbs, which speak of action at a point in the past. This speaks of the fact that the Apostle Paul had given them this information. "Received" (KJV) means "to appropriate, to receive it so as to express it." It means to bring it into the inner man.

"...and saw me doing." It is very important that what we say be shown in our lives. Pity the teacher, the preacher, the counselor who gives advice he doesn't take or preaches truth he doesn't live.

Those things we have learned, received, heard, and seen, we are to do. One of the greatest sadnesses to the heart of God is the fact that so many people in the United States give lip service to the truth of Christianity, but give so little expression to it in their lives. How it must break God's heart to see this.

I read some time ago of a rural mountain home where a

visitor found an invaluable Stradivarius violin being used to prop a door open. The family did not know its value; they just knew that it was a musical instrument. How tragic that something of such inestimable value, something so priceless could be used in such a mundane way. Perhaps this is how God feels when we take the eternal Word of God and treat it with no more respect than we would the daily newspaper. "Keep putting into practice all you learned from me."

What we dwell on, we will become. "As he thinketh in his heart, so is he" (Prov. 23:7, KJV). We must commit ourselves to dwell upon high, noble, excellent things, so that God can produce in us a character that is holy, complete, and in tune with him. When we do this, "the God of peace will be with you."

In verse 7 Paul speaks of the peace of God, and in verse 9 he speaks of the God of peace. God is a God of peace, a God of harmony, wholeness, completeness.

Content
in All
Circumstances
Philippians 4:10-13

THESE PRECIOUS VERSES speak to us about life at its very roughest point, at its greatest pressure, under the harshest circumstances, but also about how to handle life at its best. Some of us handle difficulties better than we do successes. Both are necessary. These verses talk to us about how we deal with the circumstances of life.

"How grateful I am and how I praise the Lord that you are helping me again. I know you have always been anxious to send what you could, but for a while you didn't have the chance. Not that I was ever in need, for I have learned how to get along happily whether I have much or little. I know how to live on almost nothing or with everything. I have learned the secret of contentment in every situation, whether it be a full stomach or hunger, plenty or want; for I can do everything God asks me to with the help of Christ who gives me the strength and power" (4:10-13, TLB).

Paul begins by thanking the Philippians again and telling them he has rejoiced in their care for him. Remember that the Philippian church was the main church to stand by the Apostle Paul when he came into Macedonia. They sent gifts to him. They prayed for him. They sent helpers with him to minister to him and with him. The epistle of Philippians is a very gracious "thank you" letter.

In the preceding verses Paul discussed the peace of God that surpasses all human understanding. In these verses he tells the Philippians that this peace will help them to adjust to the circumstances of life. This peace will help them deal with the problems and the difficulties, the nitty-gritty of life.

CONCERN

"How grateful I am and how I praise the Lord that you are helping me again. I know you have always been anxious to send what you could, but for a while you didn't have the chance" (4:10, TLB). "Grateful" ("rejoiced," KJV) is in the aorist tense in the Greek, which is the equivalent to our past perfect tense. Throughout the book Paul used this word in the present tense, which in essence means to rejoice and keep on rejoicing. But here he speaks of a past act of rejoicing and gratitude. He points them to a specific act of his rejoicing over their kindness. Their concern for him was now met with a specific "thank you" for what they did.

He is very careful to express appreciation for their acts of kindness. Apparently there had been a period of time when they did not have the opportunity to minister to him. Perhaps they did not know about his imprisonment for a period of days, or perhaps they were unable to send a messenger to help him because he says, "At the last your care of me hath flourished again" (KJV). The word "flourished" means "bloomed again." In other words, it lay dormant through winter as it were, but now spring has come and it is blooming again. It speaks of a tree that may lose its foliage and stand in stark barrenness in the wintertime. But spring comes and the sap flows. The life energy of that tree expresses itself with leaves and foliage. That is the word that Paul uses here to describe the Philippians' care for him. Their care was absent for a while, but now it is flourishing again. He is very quick to let them know that he does not blame them, that he does not think it was a lack of interest on their part. It would be wonderful if it could be said of us that the only reason we don't provide for each other's needs is that we don't have the opportunity. When we see the concern that is evident in this verse, we can understand why Paul loved this church so greatly. They stood with him and they provided for his needs.

Real friendship can stand the test of silence. Paul did not hear from them, but he knew they still cared, they still loved him. Their friendship with him was not dependent upon their always telling him or always reassuring him of their love and concern. The greatest friendships that I share are not the ones that I necessarily enjoy the most often. There are friends I may not see for years and years. But when we get back together, we don't have to start over again, we just take up where we left off. These verses give a beautiful picture of a relationship that can stand the pressure of silence. A lack of attention is not necessarily evidence of a lack of concern.

CONTENTMENT

"Not that I was ever in need, for I have learned how to get along happily whether I have much or little. I know how to live on almost nothing or with everything. I have learned the secret of contentment in every situation, whether it be a full stomach or hunger, plenty or want" (4:11, 12, TLB). It is obvious that what the Philippians provided for Paul met a real need in his life, and Paul wanted to thank them. But he also wanted to be sure they knew he was not trying to solicit another gift from them. "Learned" in verse 12 is a word that goes back into ancient mystical religious practice. It literally means "to be initiated into a rite." It spoke of the mystical religions of the East, and the word itself was used of someone who was initiated into the secret truths or doctrines of a mystery religion. That was its original meaning. It speaks of discipline, hardship, and of learning the key or secret.

In this context it obviously is not speaking of pagan mystery religions. Paul is saying, "I have found the secret of living. I have learned that in whatever state I am, I should be content. I have learned the secret of living above my circumstances." "Learned" speaks of secrecy, and Paul tells us what the secret is. He had learned that whatever his circumstances were, they did not have to affect his well-being or the meaning of his life. If our happiness depends on the praise of other people, wealth, possessions, or anything circumstantial, we are to be pitied. Paul had learned to live with a genuine peace in his life, regardless of the circumstances.

To be sure there is a divine discontent! Paul was not saying that he had learned to be content with everything in life. Not at all! We are not to be content with our own imperfections, the sins in our lives that continually draw us away from God. We are not to be content with the needs of those around us. We are to be concerned and discontented with those needs, so that we can meet them. We are not to be content to see men die and go to hell. There ought to always be a tension between what we are and what God wants us to be. But we shouldn't be unhappy just because things don't go like we want them to.

Paul was content whatever his circumstances. "I know how to live on almost nothing or with everything" (4:12, TLB). Some suffer the humiliation of poverty, of not being able to provide for the needs of life. Paul knew how to do that. The word "abound" (KJV) means "to overflow." Paul knew how to have more than he needed too. He had been in both places.

The Apostle Paul was raised in a very rich, aristocratic family. He was born with a silver spoon in his mouth. He had plenty of everything when he was young. After he gave his heart to Christ and began to preach, there came a time in his life when he suffered poverty. He knew what it was like to be hungry, to not have a place to stay, to not have clothing. He understood. He knew how to be humiliated in poverty and he knew how to have everything.

The word "know" is used in an unusual way. It means "to understand." We know how we are supposed to act in poverty and we know how we are supposed to act in affluence. But Paul says that he *understood* it. Do we understand our poverty? Do we understand our wealth? Do we understand the responsibility it places upon us? It is one thing to accept intellectually the facts in our mind of how we are to act, but do we understand the tremendous responsibility and opportunity poverty and wealth afford?

The greatest witness Christianity has ever had has been by those whose circumstances were less than what they really needed for life. In that time they trusted God and gave a witness for him which he blessed. Most of us know how to be abased. As soon as a problem comes, we run to Jesus. But few of us know how to abound. Prosperity has destroyed far more Christians than adversity ever has. If we are people of privilege who abound, who overflow, who have more than we need day by day, we have a tremendous opportunity to understand what that means and how we are to act.

CONQUEST
"I can do everything God asks me to with the help of Christ who gives me the strength and power" (4:13, TLB).

The emphasis here is upon "everything." In all of Paul's contentment with his circumstances, in all of his understanding of abasement and abundance, in all of his understanding of what it means to live in fellowship with God, the key was Jesus Christ. The Stoics and the Greek philosophers said that a man ought to be self-sufficient; he ought to have the answer within himself. The Apostle Paul, using the same words that the Stoics and philosophers used, said that the answer was within him; but it was Jesus in him, not himself. It was not self-sufficiency; it was Christ-confidence. It was Jesus' strength, Jesus' intellect in him that accomplished his contentment. Strength and power was transmitted from Jesus to Paul.

Haven't we all observed the beauty of nature, perhaps in viewing the Grand Canyon or watching a man walk on the moon, and thought, "Isn't our God great! Isn't our God magnificent!" But when we look at nature we have not seen the greatest power of God. The greatest power of God is transmitted from Christ to us. Many stare at the heavens and say, "What a great God we have." But God wants us to be able to look inside and say, "What a great God we have." It is not the power of a roll of thunder that demonstrates the power of God. It is the power of Jesus Christ living in a heart, causing that heart to rise above circumstances, above brokenness, above all of the things of life and have victory and conquest in the midst of it. God wants to demonstrate and reveal his power through us.

We can have the right attitude toward life, toward God, toward fellow Christians, and toward our circumstances, not because we have a good philosophy of life or a positive attitude, but because of Jesus Christ who strengthens us. Christ is the ultimate answer for life's turmoil. If we depend upon our ideals, our philosophy of life, our attitudes, sooner or later there will come an experience that will shatter every ideal we have built up, every philosophy which we have believed. But if our strength and our power have been transmitted to us from Christ and it is his life within us, no circumstance can destroy his power within us. We can do everything through Christ who strengthens us.

How do we have that kind of strength? We do not have it by being casual about our faith. We do not have it by being compromising or disobedient. The way to lay hold of the power of God is to obey God. Each time we obey him, another door is opened and another understanding is reached. As we go from step to step, from obedience to obedience, from faith to faith, we are able to have God transmit into us the very power of his presence. Then we too will be initiated into the secret of contentment in all circumstances and victory through the power of Christ in our lives.

**Profit
to Your
Account**
Philippians 4:14-19

THE BOOK OF Philippians is a letter from the Apostle Paul to his favorite church. It was not a rich church. It did not abound in prominent, wealthy people. Paul talks about this church in 2 Corinthians: "Now I want to tell you what God in his grace has done for the churches in Macedonia. Though they have been going through much trouble and hard times, they have mixed their wonderful joy with their deep poverty, and the result has been an overflow of giving to others" (2 Cor. 8:1, 2, TLB). It was poor, but generous. It was not wealthy by men's standards, but it generously gave out of its poverty.

This is the church to which the Apostle Paul is writing to give instructions. In this passage he talks to them about their giving and their involvement in the ministry of the gospel. "But even so, you have done right in helping me in my present difficulty. As you well know, when I first brought the Gospel to you and then went on my way, leaving Macedonia, only you Philippians became my partners in giving and receiving. No other church did this. Even when I was over in Thessalonica you sent help twice. But though I appreciate your gifts, what makes me happiest is the well-earned reward you will have because of your kindness. At the moment I have all I need—more than I need! I am generously supplied with the gifts you sent me when Epaphroditus came. They are a sweet-smelling sacrifice that pleases God well. And it is he who will supply all your needs from his riches in glory, because of what Christ Jesus has done for us" (4:14-19, TLB).

"But even so, you have done right." The Greek word translated "done right" means "immediately, when one looked at it, it appeared to be good." They did it and immediately saw it was a good thing. This word also indicates that the good thing which is done secures for the person a share in something else. This is the key that runs throughout this passage of Scripture. These Christians in Philippi had shared their possessions, their love, their hearts, their ministry with the Apostle Paul and with others who were spreading the gospel.

We need to see the truth that is involved here because it is the key for our understanding of the real meaning of biblical stewardship as it relates to our possessions.

INVESTMENT MADE

The Philippians' help was not an investment made to return to them interest on the dollar, but it did pay rich dividends. Do not think for a moment that God is going to let us give more to him than he gives to us. It cannot happen.

"You have done right in helping me in my present difficulty." "Helping" is a form of *koinonia,* a word that runs throughout the New Testament. It means "fellowship" or "partnership." He is saying to them, "You did a good thing, because you became partners with me in the ministry of the gospel. You gave of your possessions, and so we became partners in this enterprise."

The words he uses in these next verses are financial terms, terms we would expect to find in a bank or in a financial institution. They indicate that a partnership has been formed. There is a debit, a credit, a receipt in full, and interest compounded. These are the words used to describe this investment.

When we share that which God has entrusted to us, whether it be the love of our hearts, our possessions, or whatever, we actually become partners with those to whom we give. Those with whom we link our lives form a partnership with us. "You have now made an investment, you have joined an alliance, you have made a partnership with me," Paul is saying.

"As you well know, when I first brought the Gospel to you and then went on my way, leaving Macedonia, only you Philippians became my partners in giving and receiving. No other church did this" (4:15, TLB). This is debit and credit, collection and accounting, accounts payable and accounts receivable. He identifies Thessalonica as the place where he received their gifts (4:16). Thessalonica was a very wealthy, prominent city; yet these poor people in Philippi gave to help the people in Thessalonica. Those in poverty gave to those in the country clubs. The Philippians were poor, and yet they gave and received as they gave. Paul said of them, "They gave not only what they could afford, but far more" (2 Cor. 8:3, TLB). If we only give what we think we can afford, we will never do what we ought to do in stewardship. We will never test the resources of God. We must come to the place where we give out of God's resources, so God can give to us out of his resources. If we only give according to what we tally up on our sheet as a good return to God, we will cheat ourselves because we never get down to being involved in eternal giving and receiving.

The Philippians believers gave themselves to the Lord and to Paul. They gave out of their poverty and suffering. As a result they received great joy. They invested in Paul. When we give, it is God's way of meeting needs for others. When we give and God uses it to meet the needs of someone else, a giving cycle is begun that is not completed until it has returned to us in the form of joy and blessings. It may return to us in financial blessings. It may return to us in a way that is strictly a happiness that defies every circumstance we have and a peace that cannot be gained any other way. Any time we fail to give out of God's resources, we cut the cycle and stop the flow of the blessings of God, not only to others, but to ourselves.

INTEREST MEASURED

"But though I appreciate your gifts, what makes me happiest is the well-earned reward you will have because of your kindness" (4:17, TLB). "Desire" (KJV) is a word that means "to search after, to seek for." It is a restless hunting for something. Paul says that he doesn't have a desire for their gifts. He appreciates them, but he is not asking for their money. "What makes me happiest is the well-earned reward you will have." He is searching earnestly that they may receive eternal interest on their gifts. We will receive even as we invest.

That is true financially today. It is unrealistic for us to go to the bank and ask for interest on $10,000 if we don't have $10,000 on deposit. The same thing is true spiritually, in our partnership with God's people and with the purposes of God. We must invest if we are to receive interest. We must put on deposit if there is to be an interest compounded. These are again financial terms, and the words "well-earned reward" mean that interest may be compounded to our account. God *does* pay interest. Jesus answered his disciples, when they asked him what they would get from following him, "Anyone who gives up his home, brothers, sisters, father, mother, wife, children, or property, to follow me shall receive a hundred times as much in return, and shall have eternal life" (Matt. 19:29,

TLB). "A hundred times as much" is 10,000 percent interest.

We will receive interest on what we deposit, what we invest. We will get back what we have entrusted to God. Paul is saying, "I am not trying to get something for me, but I want you to have profit to your account, fruit that will be credited to you."

Paul's real joy was not what the gift did for him, but what the gift did for them. It provided for his need, but it allowed them to get in on the giving cycle of eternity, to receive out of God's riches. He was happy for them because of what they would receive as a result of their gift.

No gift which we make to God ever leaves us poorer! God will never be in debt to us. Paul was rejoicing in the Philippian's gifts to him because they were recipients of the gifts of God.

INCREASE MANIFESTED

"At the moment I have all I need—more than I need! I am generously supplied with the gifts you sent me when Epaphroditus came. They are a sweet-smelling sacrifice that pleases God well" (4:18, TLB). In the Old Testament the priests would bring the sacrifice to the altar and present it to God. When the aroma of the sacrifice made its way to the heavens, then the priest would turn to the people and reveal to them that the sacrifice had been acceptable to God. Paul is drawing upon that figure here. He is saying, "You sent me a gift. I brought it to God and placed it upon the altar. As the aroma of your sacrifice ascended to heaven, God was well-pleased with it. God accepted it. God was happy with what you have done." That is the ultimate desire of the real Christian, to have our lives approved and acceptable and pleasing unto God.

"I have all" (4:18) is a financial word which means "I

have been paid in full." It is as though he was saying, "I give you a receipt in full. I labored among you with the gospel, and you have now presented to me a gift which settles the account in full. I have an overflowing life because of what you have done."

When we can measure every spiritual experience and every commitment we make as part of our gifts to God, and if the desire of our hearts is that we may be pleasing to God, he will manifest himself in our lives in an abundant and overflowing way. Are we pleasing God in our living? Are we pleasing God in our giving? Are we pleasing God in our relationship with him?

INFLATION MET

Our needs have a way of getting exaggerated. I don't know much about finances, but I do know that my dollar does not go as far as it once did. This means that there is a greater necessity. Notice what Paul says about meeting inflation: "And it is he who will supply all your needs from his riches in glory, because of what Christ Jesus has done for us" (4:19, TLB). The Philippians provided for Paul's needs, and now theirs would be provided by God. God would give to them out of his riches because they gave out of their poverty. They gave what had been entrusted to them, and now God would respond to their poverty with eternal riches. "Supply" is a word which literally means, "fill up something that is empty." Whatever emptiness there may be in their lives, God will fill it. They had "a great trial of affliction" and "deep poverty" (2 Cor. 8:1, 2, KJV). But God filled them completely and fully.

We can know today that whatever our needs are, God will provide for them. As we bring our empty vessels, whatever they may be, God fills them. Whether it is the need for forgiveness, the need for peace and comfort, the need for guidance and direction, the need for the necessities of life, God shall supply all of our needs. Nothing is beyond his providence or concern. Nothing we need is beyond his power to give to us.

And he does it "from his riches." If someone is going to take care of us, we certainly want to know they have the resources to do it. Whatever we need God can provide.

It is tragic that we never trust God enough to test his resources. It is tragic that we give out of *our* abundance instead of God's. We ought to give sacrificially, and when we do God is committed to take care of us.

We do not have the joy that God wants to give until we have given like that. Christian ministries do not need our money. But, we desperately need to give it. Some of us have robbed and cheated God with our gifts. We have committed crimes against eternity, and we have wondered why God doesn't bless us. We wonder why our families have fallen apart and our businesses have turned sour. We wonder why we come to church and are not blessed. It is because we give out of our abundance, not out of our poverty. Most of us spend more money every week on incidentals than we give to the cause of Christ. How can God bless that? We need to learn that when we give as God prompts—out of our poverty, out of our need—then God is going to give to us out of his riches through Jesus Christ. He wants to bless us and we won't let him. We don't have enough faith to do it. Thus, we are in no position to be spiritual leaders because we are not depending on God's resources.

Because of what we do in response to the needs of the world, God takes our investment, compounds the interest, and fills our every need out of his riches. God's bank will never go bankrupt. There will never be an experience that we face that God is not adequate to meet, but we have to believe God and commit ourselves to him. Our gifts must come out of the deep commitment of our hearts to Jesus Christ.

Basically we do not give as we ought because we don't love God as we ought. We have not fully committed our lives to him. We should give out of our need because he is compounding the interest. He will give it back. It may come in the form of dollars if that is what we need. It may come in the form of a deep peace in our heart which we don't have now and desperately need. It may come in the form of freedom from guilt which hangs like a shroud over our souls. But we give to God our love, our worship, our commitment, our possessions, whatever he has given to us, and he will return it to us.

26

Saints
in Caesar's
Household
Philippians 4:20-23

"NOW UNTO GOD our Father be glory forever and ever. Amen. Sincerely, Paul. P.S. Say 'hello' for me to all the Christians there; the brothers with me send their greetings too. And all the other Christians here want to be remembered to you, especially those who work in Caesar's palace. The blessings of our Lord Jesus Christ be upon your spirits" (4:20-23, TLB).

GLORY

The reason for Paul's gratitude was that God may receive glory. The reason for the Philippians' gifts to the Apostle Paul was so God could receive glory. The reason for their love for each other and their unity in the Spirit was so God would be glorified. Very simply, the purpose for our lives is to give glory to God (4:20). That is why we are here. That is why God has given us life.

Paul concludes this epistle by ascribing to God the glory that ought to come to him. If we could live in the light and understanding that our lives in every way are to give glory to God, it would greatly affect the things we do, the things we say, the relationships that we have. God must be glorified.

GREETINGS

Paul gives three greetings in these two verses and underscores several important things for us. The King James
Version says, "Salute every saint in Christ Jesus" (4:21).
Our greetings and our relationships together are *in* the
Lord. What these greetings do is to lift the things that we
normally give the least thought to into a perspective of real
significance. We do not give much thought to what we say
when we greet each other, but there ought to be something distinctive about the way a Christian says "hello."
The thing that influences lost people toward the gospel
more than anything else is not our discipline, but our
graciousness, our love, our winsomeness. We should
greet each other in the Lord, lifting our casual greetings
into a whole new perspective. Even casual encounters are
significant encounters.

The King James Version refers to "saints." Every child
of God has the right to that title. But the word "saint"
comes from a root in the original language which means
"holy." That is a reminder to us of the high privilege and
responsibility of holy living. We are to greet each other in a
way that sets us apart. We ought to be different in every
relationship we have.

"And all the other Christians here want to be remembered to you, especially those who work in Caesar's
palace" (4:22, TLB). That is one of the most intriguing
verses in the New Testament. "Caesar's palace" refers to
all who worked within the employ or the supervision of
the emperor. That could refer to people all over the Roman
Empire, but specifically it applied to those who worked in
the emperor's palace in Rome.

The emperor was Nero, one of the most ruthless, vicious men who ever ruled the world. Normally those who
lived in the palace of such an evil king would take on his
bad habits of immorality and blasphemy. But here we see

a band of Christians at the heart of one of the most wicked places in the world.

Here was goodness in an unexpected place, as though a clean, clear river flowed from a muddy, poisonous spring. Where would the gospel have more influence than in a place like that? If the gospel could find root in Nero's palace, it could spread all around the world, which indeed it did. These Christians in Caesar's household were saints of great courage, for it took tremendous boldness to stand for Christ in that kind of atmosphere. If they didn't really love God and if they hadn't really committed themselves to Christ, they never would have made it.

Do we find that we are having a hard time developing our spiritual lives? Do we find that there are pressures brought to bear on us that make it difficult to grow in the Lord? Take heart, for even in Nero's palace the gospel found root and flourished and grew. There are some situations and circumstances where it is easier to develop spiritual life than others, but spiritual life can be developed anywhere. It is an encouraging thing to know that here in the center of a pagan empire, there was a colony of Christians who though they were oppressed and their courage often tested stood for Christ. And their witness was a blessing to the entire world.

GRACE

"The grace of our Lord Jesus Christ be upon you all. Amen" (4:23, KJV). Grace is not something we earn by our goodness or our efforts. It is given as the spontaneous gift of God. Grace is freely bestowed; we do not deserve it.

The original language says, "The grace of our Lord Jesus Christ be with your spirit." It is interesting that the word "spirit" is singular. We would expect that since he is talking about all these people, he would refer to their "spirits." But he says "spirit." This is a further testimony of the oneness of heart and the oneness of spirit that characterized this great church. It was a church of people who lived to honor God and to see the gospel furthered. It was a generous and unselfish church. It was a church that loved the Lord and stood upon the principles of the Word of God. It was united in heart, purpose, and mind so that when the Apostle Paul got ready to tell them "good-bye," "God bless you," he used the singular. He spoke as though all of them were one. That is the intent and purpose of God for his people, that they be knit together as one. Only the grace of God makes this possible. Only God's grace can so blend our hearts together.